PRAISE FOR
MADISON AVENUE MANSLAUGHTER

Jon Bond, CEO Tomorro; former CEO, Big Fuel; co-founder,
Kirshenbaum Bond & Partners.
"*It isn't* manslaughter, *it's industry* suicide *in slow motion, one FTE at a time.*"

Brian Sheehan, Associate Professor of Advertising, Newhouse School,
Syracuse University; former Chairman and CEO, Team One.
"*Michael Farmer's book is a deeply insightful probe into the declining financial
and creative positions of advertising agencies around the world. He uncovers basic
issues that few in the industry are admitting to, or even talking about. Unless these
issues are addressed with some urgency, agencies, holding companies and clients will
continue to suffer. Together, they should follow Farmer's advice.*"

Tim Williams, Founder and Managing Director, Ignition Consulting Group.
"*Michael Farmer details the devolution of advertising agencies from highly-
profitable, highly-valued business partners to their current state as undervalued
service providers. Fortunately, he also prescribes a bevy of solutions that will help the
agency industry regain its rightful place in the business world, which involves not
just helping them change their practices, but most importantly their beliefs.*"

Richard Roth, President and Founder, Roth Observatory.
"*Finally someone has written a book about everything I believe in. Farmer
identifies the causes and dynamics of the industry's issues and woes. He understands
the economics, the behaviors and the causes of an inevitable talent drain. Solutions
are scarce and they require a keen understanding of the business. Farmer has this
understanding.*"

MADISON AVENUE

MANSLAUGHTER

AN INSIDE VIEW OF FEE-CUTTING CLIENTS,
PROFIT-HUNGRY OWNERS AND DECLINING AD AGENCIES

Published by
LID Publishing Ltd
Garden Studios, 71-75 Shelton Street
Covent Garden, London WC2H 9JQ

31 West 34th Street, Suite 8004,
New York, NY 10001, US

info@lidpublishing.com
www.lidpublishing.com

A member of:

BPR
Business Publishers Roundtable

www.businesspublishersroundtable.com

Printed in Great Britain by TJ International
ISBN: 978-0-9860793-0-6

Cover and page design: Laura Hawkins

MADISON AVENUE MANSLAUGHTER

MANSLAUGHTER

AN INSIDE VIEW OF FEE-CUTTING CLIENTS, PROFIT-HUNGRY OWNERS AND DECLINING AD AGENCIES

MICHAEL FARMER

FOREWORD BY
KEVIN ROBERTS
EXECUTIVE CHAIRMAN OF SAATCHI & SAATCHI

LONDON   MONTERREY
MADRID   SHANGHAI
MEXICO CITY   BOGOTA
NEW YORK   BUENOS AIRES
BARCELONA   SAN FRANCISCO

For **JO ANN**
COLIN, ALEX *and* **TAYLOR**

In order to arrive there,
To arrive where you are, to get to where you are not,
You must go by a way wherein there is no ecstasy.
In order to arrive at what you do not know
You must go by a way which is the way of ignorance.
In order to possess what you do not possess
You must go by the way of dispossession.
In order to arrive at what you are not
You must go through the way in which you are not.
And what you do not know is the only thing you know
And what you own is what you do not own
And where you are is where you are not.

T.S. ELIOT

TABLE OF CONTENTS

FOREWORD

We live in a VUCA world.

A world that is Volatile, Uncertain, Complex and Ambiguous. Everything is changing at warp-speed. Technology is changing the way we live, work and play in new ways every day. Power is shifting from the Established to the New to the Who would ever have imagined! The Power Train has shifted from Manufacturers to Brands, from Brands to the Media, from the Media to the Retailer, and now from the Retailer to We the People. We are all demanding More for Less and we want it Now. All of it. Better. Cheaper and Faster. And it must be Irresistible not Interruptive. Chaos, Connectivity and Collaboration are the New Normal. All powered by Creativity. All powered by an Idea.

And right in the middle of this seismic change are the Communicators. The conduit between the Manufacturers, the Retailers and their Customers and Consumers - the Advertising Agency. And boy oh boy, are we struggling to keep up, let alone get ahead.

We are sailing in a Red Sea of blood, (mainly ours!). A Red Sea of time pressure, talent exodus to the New Age Tech darlings, demanding, short-term results driven clients, antiquated systems and processes, and increasing competition in every part of our traditional business. All under the umbrella of it's no longer good enough to offer two out of three. (You can have two of Great, Fast and Cheap and two only.) Clients demand all three.

How can we, the Advertising Agencies, leave this Sea of Red and set sail for new Blue Seas, new blue skies?

Not without transformational and dramatic change.

Not by anything starting with Re. Restructuring, re-engineering, reframing will not cut it.

The Industry must forsake its historical penchant for tinkering and incremental change, and transform itself for the first time in 100 years.

This book spells out the Unpleasant Realities and the Unvarnished Truth of what needs to be done.

It pulls no punches.

It puts the onus on Agency leaders to define their own destiny and chart their own course from Red Seas to Blue.

It calls for transformation of the way agencies staff, do work and charge for that work.

It turns many 'Industry norms' upside down.

It can be ugly and uncomfortable at times.

But it does tell the Unvarnished Truth

KEVIN ROBERTS,
EXECUTIVE CHAIRMAN,
SAATCHI & SAATCHI

EXECUTIVE SUMMARY

The post-World War II growth of advertising agencies is one of the world's great business success stories. Television advertising became a dominant force, and ad agencies were paid via 15% media commissions. The high status and profitability of ad agencies during this period allowed agencies to expand globally, manage themselves loosely and go public in the '60s and '70s.

Ad agencies were subsequently acquired by marketing communications holding companies, and the holding companies themselves grew and showed a track record of increased profits as they continued to acquire agencies and generate bottom-line growth by reducing agency costs. By 1990, their agencies were "at the top of their game," buoyed by inflating media prices that boosted commission income, and their profitable record of success locked in their vision of what they needed to do to stay successful – keep on focusing on creativity and client service.

Today, though, the operating and financial health of ad agencies has reversed and is weakening. The commission system disappeared in the '80s and '90s, replaced by fees managed downwards by procurement executives who believed that agencies were high cost suppliers whose value-added was overstated. Clients instituted global marketing practices that put pressure on agency operations and raised their costs. Management consultants displaced senior agency executives as CEO advisors in response to the new corporate "shareholder value" mantra. Ad agencies became viewed by their clients as commodity suppliers of creative services, easily replaced through agency searches, and the length of client relationships diminished substantially. Digital and social marketing innovations added specialized agency competitors to the mix of agencies servicing advertisers, and scopes of work expanded significantly at a time when agencies were downsizing in response to fee pressures. Agencies became trapped between low client fees and growing workloads while having to deliver growing margins to their holding company owners. Capabilities were reduced at a time when clients' expectations for increased digital / social know-how and improved results were at a feverish pitch.

The declining fortunes of ad agencies are not visible to those who follow holding company income and profit growth, since ad agencies continue to fuel holding company margins – but they do this the hard way, by squeezing their resources and holding the line on salaries and bonuses. This is a game that will, sooner rather than later, get played out with unhappy consequences for all.

This is Michael Farmer's diagnosis of the strategic problems facing advertising agencies and outlined in *Madison Avenue Manslaughter.* Farmer, who has worked with ad agencies and their clients since 1992, has a unique strategic understanding of agency scopes of work, and he has tied together an understanding of industry workloads, fees and resources that forms the economic foundation of this book.

Agencies do not document, measure or track their workloads – they focus on being creative, winning awards, delivering service, and generating profit margins. They have little understanding of the growing gap among their workloads, fees and resources. Consequently, senior advertising executives like agency CEOs misdiagnose the strategic problems facing their agencies and fail to mobilize their organizations to respond effectively.

This lack of knowledge makes it easier for CEOs to respond to agency profit problems by downsizing. If workload sizes and growth rates were known, CEOs would certainly pause before downsizing to generate profit margins for holding company owners.

Agencies have not changed their internal cultures in response to these changing circumstances. Loose management practices dominate agency cultures, just as they did during the high-profit past. Client heads are not held accountable for depressed fee levels, unmanaged workloads or insufficient resources for client work. Office heads are not held accountable for the varied performance of their client heads.

Agencies are on a path to self-destruction. Thus far, the level of senior executive response to this problem has been surprisingly weak. Through benign

13

neglect of growing creative workloads, and reluctance to tackle clients over declining client fees, agency CEOs are presiding over the slow decline and over-stretching of a diminishing pool of burned-out creative assets. Efforts to develop new clients and grow revenue is their most visible response to client fee pressures, but since every ad agency CEO is going down the same path, this approach leads to further-depressed industry prices that make their situations worse.

Agencies need strong CEO leaders who are prepared to grapple with three clear challenges:

1.   **The workload challenge**. Agencies must begin to document, track and measure their workloads. This will permit their organizations to do a much more effective job negotiating fees and closing the gap between workloads and fees. This will require new policies, new tools and a new sense of organizational discipline.

2.   **The mission challenge**. This involves rethinking and then repositioning the *raison d'être* of the agency from "creativity and service" to "results for clients." Only through such a repositioning can agencies begin to set course for higher fees (as measured by billing multiples), begin to close the "value-added gap" between themselves and the management consulting firms, and identify with their clients' need for increased shareholder value. This cannot be done without a wholesale upgrading of skills, particularly in client service and strategic planning, so training is a key part of the required mix.

3.   **The accountability challenge**. The third challenge involves running the agency like a business and creating a strong sense of accountability throughout the organization, especially by office heads and their client heads. The current loose structure, based on the principle that *"everyone thinks they know what needs to be done, and they do it without management's knowledge or involvement"* was possible when agencies earned very high levels of commission income, but it is inappropriate today and cannot be justified romantically on the basis of *"this is what is required to run a creative*

organization." Increased accountability will require measures, objectives and management reviews to evaluate client-by-client and agency executive performance relative to established goals and targets.

Madison Avenue Manslaughter describes these three challenges and lays out a detailed 10-step transformation program to be initiated by agency Chief Executive Officers who wish to restore organizational health, financial well-being and renewed strategic relevance for their ad agencies.

ACKNOWLEDGEMENTS

This work summarizes my 25 years' of experience working as a management consultant and software provider to advertising agencies and advertisers around the world.

I owe a great deal of thanks to the many senior agency executives, procurement executives and marketing executives who called on Farmer & Company to help solve the various workload, fee, resource and relationship problems that they experienced.

Each consulting engagement provided new insights about changing industry and relationship problems. We began in 1990 when agency remuneration was high and scopes of work were relatively simple. Agencies had enough income to staff their work lavishly with talented and well-paid senior and junior people, and this led to the development of high quality brand strategic work and creative ads that improved the competitiveness of advertisers' brands.

As time progressed, though, this comfortable situation frayed at the edges. Remuneration per client declined; marketing became more global; digital innovations disrupted traditional media; brands came under increased competitive pressures and agencies had to struggle to hold on to long-term clients and generate profits for holding company owners. This struggle led to downsizings and salary/bonus constraints that severely limited agency capabilities.

We observed this step by step with our clients, seeing the pieces of an industry puzzle emerge over time.

This book is an attempt to pull the pieces of the puzzle together, and to create a picture of the advertising industry that represents the collective experience of those who lived through it and continue to struggle with it today.

I owe a particular debt of gratitude to Sir Martin Sorrell, who in 1989, was the first advertising executive I met. He generously introduced me to many key advertising executives, and we were fortunate enough to begin our agency consulting practice with a WPP agency. Later, Jonathan Hirst, John Shannon, Carolyn Carter and Ed Meyer provided leadership and guidance as we worked with Grey Worldwide in various parts of the world.

Tom Rosenwald, a prominent executive search consultant, introduced me to every senior agency and holding company executive in the US after 2001, and eventually through his efforts and the help of others, we expanded our consulting practice in the US to include advertisers Hershey, Ford, Toyota, Mazda, Volvo, Kraft, American Express, Genworth, Merck, Eli Lilly, Best Buy, JC Penney, British Petroleum, Ritz-Carlton, Kayak, MasterCard and McDonald's; and agencies O&M, Y&R, Grey, JWT, DDB, BBDO, TBWA, Organic, Saatchi & Saatchi, Team One, Leo Burnett, McCann Erickson, FCB, The Martin Agency, Doner, Alma, IW Group, Burrell, Translation, Lloyd & Company and Juice Pharma.

I am indebted to Kevin Roberts, Executive Chairman of Saatchi & Saatchi, who encouraged me to finish this book and who read various drafts and offered sound words of advice, along with writing the Foreword. Kevin is a well-known industry author (Lovemarks) and one of the world's foremost Mad Men, so his support was especially valued. Bob Seelert, Bill Cochrane, Vaughan Emsley, Brent Smart and Anna Binninger of Saatchi & Saatchi were helpful in many ways; I'm grateful as well to Gary Lee, Laura Turano and Jean-Marie Le Nail of McCann Erickson; Neil Miller of FCB; Andrew Robertson and Dana Perry of BBDO; Pete Swiecicki of Omnicom; Ian Marlowe of Publicis (previously of TBWA); Alain Rhoné, Neal Grossman and Denis Streiff of TBWA; Chris Sweetland and Rick Brook of WPP; Mike Walsh, Steve Goldstein, Ralph Clementson, and Toby Drummond of O&M; Bob Jeffrey, Lew Trencher, Keith Wilkins and Mike Byrne of J Walter Thompson; Dick Roth of Roth Observatory; Deborah Wahl of McDonald's; Kristen Simmons of Experian; Debo-

rah Hedgecock of MasterCard; Mary Ann Brennan of Mattel; Jon Bond
of Tomorro (previously co-founder of Kirshenbaum Bond & Partners);
Brian Sheehan, Associate Professor of Advertising at the Newhouse
School of Syracuse University (previously CEO of ad agency Team
One); Walter Kiechel, author of The Lords of Strategy; Jim Singer of
AT Kearney; Tom Finneran of the 4A's; Bill Bain and Ralph Willard,
previously of Bain & Company; Steve Schaubert and Chris Zook of Bain &
Company; Ken Thuerbach; Kirsten Sandberg; Bob Whittington; Joe Burton
and Brian Lipton.

Many fine individuals made contributions to Farmer & Company's adver-
tising consulting practice during the past 25 years. I am grateful to Nuri
Toker, David Barrett, Nick Ford, Alistair Stranack, Virginia Eastman,
James Wolcott, Chris Tidswell (who sadly passed away in 2010), Willow
Duttge, Michelle Miller, Jennifer Stingle, Julia Schwartz, Marina Bordin,
Cameron Jones, Daniel Bellis, Ethan Dennison, Jim Stillman, Brian Suckie
and Antonio Lupo.

This strategic assessment of the highly stressed advertising industry is not
meant, in any way, to criticize or stigmatize individual agencies or executives who provided the various pieces of the industry puzzle described
in these pages. My narrative has not given full credit to the senior agency
executives who understand their strategic situation and are working very
hard to deal with it.

I am solely responsible for the conclusions in this book, and for any errors
or omissions therein.

INTRODUCTION

"Where is Madison Avenue? You might well ask."

The global growth and influence of advertising agencies is one of the world's great business success stories. From modest beginnings, the industry has grown and flourished.

Early advertising involved little more than preparing posters or running display ads in newspapers for patent medicines, soaps, cereals and cigarettes. Today, advertising blankets the world via television, movies, magazines, billboards, radio, newspapers, brochures, electronic displays, computer screens, mobile telephones – as well as via T-shirts, coffee mugs, pencils, athletic uniforms and anything else that can either catch the eye or be handed out. Digital and social advertising includes web pages, games, YouTube videos and tweets that are designed to create involvement with customers. An Oreo cookie tweet (*"You can still dunk in the dark"*) during the accidental lighting failure of the 2013 Super Bowl defined a new form of instantaneous event-driven advertising. Coca-Cola's YouTube video of drones delivering cases of Coca-Cola to immigrant high-rise construction workers in Singapore illustrated another type of innovative video advertising in the digital age.

Advertising reaches out to consumers not only from Madison Avenue, USA, but also from London, Frankfurt, Paris, Moscow, Johannesburg, Tokyo, Ho Chi Minh City, Bangkok, Beijing, Singapore, Melbourne and hundreds of other cities around the world. Advertising is ubiquitous, and so are the agencies that create it. Ogilvy & Mather, a typical global agency, shows 450 offices on its website.

Historians of advertising mark the end of World War II as the beginning of the global boom in advertising. This was The Golden Age of Advertising, when Bill Bernbach, David Ogilvy, George Lois, Leo Burnett and other well-known giants – typically founders of their firms – made enduring creative marks on the industry. They launched what came to be known as the Creative Revolution, abandoning the hard sell and making advertising entertaining, amusing and palatable. They did this through irony – making fun of advertising and having fun with the products they advertised, treating the consumer as an insider, in on their joke. Not coincidentally, the leading products they advertised grew and established strong competitive market positions, backed by large spends on over-the-air and print media that were promoted by their ad agencies, who were remunerated by commissions on the media and production spends.

Creative Revolution advertising fueled product growth and created memorable ads during the decades after World War II. It remains the template for today's advertising. Agencies, advertisers and consumers expect advertising to surprise, enlighten, and entertain; clients expect it to generate results at the same time.

Creative advertising went global with commercial television, and advertising agencies went global as well, opening up branches around the world. Their success and profitability attracted financiers from New York, London, Paris, and Tokyo, and in a short space of time, nearly every major ad agency was acquired by one of the newly-created public holding companies in marketing communications: Interpublic, Omnicom, WPP, Publicis, Dentsu, Havas, MDC – and the holding companies themselves grew and showed a positive track record of profit growth for investors. WPP, the largest of the holding companies, had 2014 revenues of £11.5 billion ($19.0 billion), a PBIT margin of 16.7% and a market capitalization of £20 billion ($33 billion), with operating companies in advertising, media, marketing data, public relations, branding, healthcare, direct, digital, promotions, and specialist communications.

Despite this holding company success, the operating and financial health of the industry's major advertising agencies is weakening. Agency weakness is neither a matter of public knowledge nor the focus of sufficient senior executive action to reverse the trend. Agencies are being squeezed, caught between reduced client fees and growing workloads[1] while having to deliver growing margins to their owners. The only way agencies can handle this conflict is to downsize[2] or otherwise adjust their headcounts and costs. This enfeebles the agencies at a time when clients' expectations for more creativity, increased digital and improved results are at a feverish pitch. Client dissatisfaction with their agencies appears to be at a high if we judge this by the rate at which they fire their current agencies and search for new ones.[3]

Agency creative workloads are growing substantially, particularly as advertisers experiment with digital and social advertising while maintaining the growth of traditional advertising comprising TV, print, radio and outdoors. With growing workloads and declining fees, agencies have to do more work with fewer, lower-cost creative people. The effort puts a considerable strain on operations and quality. Every year the strain gets worse, and agencies are becoming increasingly stretched and creatively challenged.

A sensible person might assume that agencies are paid by their clients for the work they do. This is not actually the case. Agencies are paid by the head for the number of staff assigned to their client accounts – workload is not technically a part of the headcount equation.

As a practical measure, it's the agencies' clients who determine how many agency staff are assigned and paid for. In the typical process, clients first determine an overall fee, based on their marketing budgets, and agencies in turn assign an affordable number of people based on this figure. For example, if a large client establishes an agency fee of $10 million for the coming fiscal year, a typical agency would assign a number of people that would add up to $4.25 million in salaries and benefits. This might involve 10 creatives and 32 other agency people in client service, strategic planning and production. After covering overheads of $4.25 million, the agency would have $1.5 million left to cover profits, or 15% – thus meeting holding company requirements.

The amount of creative work to be done during the year develops through a separate process. The creative workload "happens" as client marketing plans evolve throughout the year. Creative workloads grow independently, almost as if they were unrelated to agency resources or fees. These creative workloads are not measured or negotiated, although they are discussed in a process called "scope of work (SOW) planning," but because there are no workload metrics – no generally accepted way of quantifying creative workloads so that a required number of agency people can be assigned – the exercise is nearly meaningless from an operational standpoint. In any case, there are large differences between expected SOWs and the actual amount of creative work that is done. The 10 creatives assigned to the $10 million client might or might not be able to handle the workload comfortably. It all depends.

In the end, looking at the past 10 years, agency workloads have been growing but typical agency fees and headcounts have not. My analysis shows that workloads have been growing on the order of 2-3% on a compounded annual basis, while fees (on a constant dollar basis) have been declining by 2-3% on a compounded annual basis. These apparently small numbers have large effects. It only takes 15 years for an agency's compensation to be cut in half for an equivalent amount of work.

This workload-fee problem is not isolated to minor agencies. The big agencies, whose reputations were first made in traditional TV, print and radio, suffer the most: agencies like Ogilvy & Mather, J Walter Thompson, Y&R,

Grey, McCann Erickson, FCB, Lowe, BBDO, DDB, TBWA\Chiat\Day, Publicis, Saatchi & Saatchi and Leo Burnett, to name a few. These big-name agencies grew up with the belief that doing any and all client work was simply *part of the service*, as it was originally when they were paid, before 1990, via 15% media commissions. Since then, commissions have been abandoned as the unique form of agency payment. In its place, clients began paying agencies by the head, but this did not change the way agencies thought about servicing their clients. Any and all client work continues to be done for an agreed fee, which remains mostly fixed.

Workloads were not measured during the commission era, just as they are not measured today.

The enduring cultural legacy of the commission days left agencies without the means to measure their workloads. Instead, they were used to making do with the resources they could afford, just as they had been throughout their past, and if the resources were too few or too junior, they would soldier on in any case. They may have complained to their clients from time to time about how inadequate their fees were, but with much less seriousness than the problem actually warranted.

What could have changed their practices was the relentless decline in fees, driven by client procurement departments over the past 20 years, and the growing workloads. Fees divided by workload equals *price*, and price has been in decline for at least two decades:

Like the proverbial frog in a pot of cold water, agencies adapt to price declines as frogs adapt to a gradual increase in water temperature – it's fine until it is not, and the frog eventually dies. Agencies are on the same path as their amphibian friends unless something fundamental changes in the way agencies measure their growing workloads and negotiate their relationships and fees.

I have worked as a strategy consultant for advertising agencies and their clients for the past 25 years. This followed a previous 15 years as a consultant, first with The Boston Consulting Group and subsequently as a director of

Bain & Company. In 40 years, I've seen a lot of industry changes and nearly as much senior executive action. The advertising industry, though, is an outlier.

PRICE CURVE 1992-2014
(PRICES IN $2014 PER SMU)

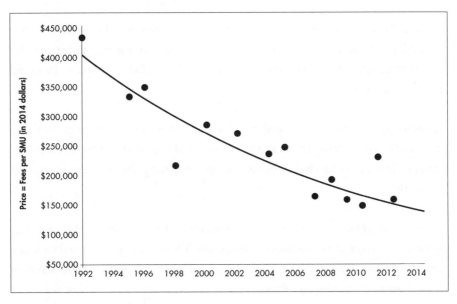

Source: Farmer & Company client data

The industry has undergone more strategic change than any other that I have seen, but the level of senior executive response to these changes has been surprisingly weak. To put it bluntly, senior agency executives have not protected their creative departments or the creative capabilities of their agencies. Through benign neglect of growing creative workloads, and reluctance to tackle clients over declining client fees, senior agency executives are presiding over the slow decline and over-stretching of a diminishing pool of burned-out creative assets. This is done in the name of meeting holding company profit expectations. Their efforts to develop new clients and grow revenues is their most visible response to client fee pressures, but since every agency CEO and president in the industry is chasing a limited pool of new business, the results are disappointing. Prices are driven even lower by cutthroat competition, and no agency manages to outgrow its competitors.

25

Jules Verne's protagonist Phileas Fogg burned his ship's furniture for fuel to reach Liverpool on his way around the world in 80 days. There is no Liverpool within reach for today's big ad agencies. The burning of creative assets is a temporary fix for a more permanent problem. At some point, the ship will find itself adrift in the middle of the ocean with no more fuel to propel it.

In this book, I outline the reasons why I believe the industry has reached a critical, even dangerous point in its development. I point out the logical consequences of the failure to act, and I'll offer a solution to avoid inevitable disaster.

Agencies and their clients need to recapture some of the respect, fun and profitability of working in what was once one of the most fulfilling and glamorous of industries but has become a grim sweatshop for the people who do the work.

Agencies complain that clients are demanding and unreasonable, and that agencies are treated as commodity suppliers. They say that it is hard to make money because fee setting is in the hands of procurement and workload is in the hands of marketing. Procurement is rewarded for lowering fees, and marketing wants to experiment, so what can be done? Agencies see a gap in perception between the value they bring and the way they are treated. They accept this as today's business reality – regrettable and unfortunate, but that's simply the way things are. A shrug of the shoulders suggests the futility of their situation.

For their part, procurement executives tend to see agencies as disorganized, chaotic and overpaid for their services. They note the annual holding company announcements of record profit levels and conclude that agencies must be much more profitable than they let on. Ad agencies have long-standing reputations for excess, fuelled especially by the annual June Festival of Creativity in Cannes. High agency fees might be acceptable if agency work were creating reliable brand growth and profitability, but brands are not exactly flourishing. Award-winning creativity is not enough; clients want improved brand performance that hits their bottom line. Agencies are not willing to be on the hook for guaranteed results. Advertisers feel entirely justified, cutting what they perceive as the fat out of agency fees.

Growing workloads and declining fees; it's a recipe for disaster. Sooner or later, an agency will embarrass its holding company and the investment community by failing to grow or deliver the necessary profits. Investment analysts will then raise questions – what has been going on?

This book was written in advance of this outcome – to outline the industry problems and encourage agencies and their clients to take management actions to keep disaster at bay. These actions form the basis of the required strategic response by agency CEOs and their clients' chief marketing and procurement officers.

SECTION I. HISTORY: THE WHEEL OF FORTUNE

Credit: Ted Goff / The New Yorker Collection / The Cartoon Bank.

A senior ad executive sat behind his desk, smiling and waving at me to sit down as he hung up the phone. He was excited: "Our third invitation to pitch this month! Things are really heating up – we're on everyone's list!"

The agency world is under constant financial pressure, and people under pressure understandably look for solutions. New business wins are seen as a big solution. The hope is that won business will add incremental revenue, offsetting lost clients and absorbing overheads, making it easier to generate profit margins for the holding companies.

Of course, every agency in the industry has the same thought, so new business pitches are highly contested. There are many new business opportunities, but only because clients are changing their agencies at more frequent rates. It's a strange kind of opportunity, because it adds more economic downside than economic upside. There is excess capacity in the industry. Competition for new business drives fees downwards, and no particular agency wins more than its fair-share of new business. In short, the new business game is just an expensive game of musical chairs, and the constant shifting of accounts from one agency to another depresses agency economics by raising costs and pushing fees down. New business wins are necessary, but the new business outcome for the industry is an economic disappointment.

The agency world has experienced many dramatic changes during the past several decades: a shift in remuneration from commission to fee; the rise of holding companies; the involvement of procurement in fee-setting; client and holding company obsession with quarterly profits; globalization of relationships; and growth of new media, especially in digital and social media, where the exploitation of "big data" is supposed to lead to new insights and increased marketing effectiveness.

All of these changes have inevitably led to declining fees, rising workloads and stretched resources. Workload growth and fee declines are strategically and economically incompatible. Tragedy is a likely outcome for financially weak agencies. This is not an industry that has unlimited potential for economies of scale or productivity increases, like the computer industry. There is no Moore's Law[4] for the advertising industry.

In the chapters that follow, I will outline the key historical events that have shaped the industry. and then propose what can and needs to be done.

CHAPTER 1 –
REMUNERATION

"Money is life's report card."

Credit: William Hamilton / The New Yorker / The Cartoon Bank.

For more than 100 years, up to the 1980s, advertisers created budgets for advertising, of which most of the costs were for media space (print) and air time (radio and television). Their agencies kept a percentage of this spend to plan and develop the associated advertising. This percentage was called a "media commission," and it was meant to cover all of the agencies' in-house costs and profits. It did not matter how many agency people were involved or how much work the agency carried out. The commission was simply a percentage of media spend, and the basis of the calculation was very straightforward. Additionally, agencies charged a mark-up on bought-in production expenses – identified, in many cases, as a "service charge" for handling production logistics (Barton, 1955, p. 9).

Most business historians attribute the commission system to agency N.W. Ayer & Sons. In 1874, N.W. Ayer implemented its "open contract," a contract with a standard media commission rate of 15 percent (N.W. Ayer & Son, 1909). The rest of the industry noticed. In 1893, the American Newspapers' Association, representing the sellers of advertising space, formally recognized agency commissions and the prevailing rate. Importantly, the Association stated that these commissions *would only be available to advertising agents, not to advertisers.* This meant that advertisers could not get an equivalent discount by buying direct from the publisher. As N.W. Ayer & Sons wrote in its self-promotional book *Forty Years of Advertising*: "The [commission system] pulled the advertising business out of the muck and mire of bidding and faking, and made the advertising agent an agent of the customer rather than an agent of any publication or group of publications" (N.W. Ayer & Son, 1909). By extension, the advertiser was now positioned as the agent's client. Advertiser-agent interests were more closely aligned than ever before.

In 1901, magazines followed the newspapers and agreed to adhere to the fixed commission system. Decades later, when radio and television came along, the 15% commission was so well established that it was accepted as a matter of course (Barton, 1955, p. 7).

A typical print transaction worked as follows:

An advertiser would request an agency to arrange for the publication of a certain advertisement in a magazine; the space would cost $1,000.

The agency would contract with the magazine publisher for the space, and the publisher would run the advertisement in that space.

The publisher would then send a bill for $850 to the agency, representing the cost of the space less the agency commission (or 15%) allowed by the publisher. The publisher agreed that he would allow an additional 2% on the $850 if the bill was paid promptly.

The agency paid the publisher $833.

The agency billed the advertiser $983, which represented the net cost of the advertising, $1,000, less the 2% cash discount, or $17, which is assumed the advertiser would earn if he paid the bill within the period of grace. The agency also billed the advertiser for the cost of the art work, photo engravings, and type composition bought by it for use in the advertisement, plus (a markup of) 15% as a service charge.

The advertiser remitted $983 to the agency to cover the cost of magazine space, and repaid the agency for the amount spent for artwork and production plus 15% of this amount as a service charge for handling the purchases

(Barton, 1955, pp. 8-9).

In 1917, the commission system got one of its strongest lobbyists, the American Association of Advertising Agencies (4A's). In a statement later attributed to the 4A's, the association argued that the 15% commission standard was the *lifeblood of the advertising agency.* Without it, 4A's argued, agencies would die a slow and painful death. A fee system would only encourage competition on price, and price-cutting would see agencies give less and less service to advertisers. If agencies did not have to compete on price, the only question advertisers would have to decide was "which agency will give the best and most service" (Haase, 1934, p. 128).

Advertisers, on the other hand, were disenchanted with commissions. In 1934, Albert E. Haase wrote a paper for the Association of National Advertisers (ANA), bashing the practice of fixed commissions and calling the practice out-of-date. Fixed commissions were simply the "easiest way for agencies to keep getting paid," he argued. Furthermore, there was no relation between the agency's task and the remuneration it received, and commissions encouraged agencies to prioritize one medium over another based on potential income. Finally, it was unfair for agencies to buy space in publications at a discount when advertisers could not (Haase, 1934, p. 60).

It would take a few decades for the balance to tip in the direction of ANA, away from commissions in the direction of labor-based fees. In the meantime, remuneration during the commission era was very high relative to the amount of work to be done and costs of the agency people required for the work. Clients were aware of this, of course, since they could see that agencies were both exceptionally well-paid and ostentatious about it. Anyone working as an account person could buy an expensive lunch any time for anyone, reported Martin Mayer in *Madison Avenue USA* (Mayer, 1959, p. 9). There were in-agency bars, private chefs, first-class travel, town cars, and pricey décor:

- J Walter Thompson in 1958 had more than one hundred private offices decorated to the tastes of the individual – one vice chairman for example had a round gaming table with cups for chips in his office. The agency maintained an executive dining suite composed of an 18th century farmhouse from Ipswich, Mass. which the agency purchased in 1920 and reconstructed in its headquarters building.

- In the mid-1960s, the Interpublic Group of Companies, parent of McCann Erickson, owned a fleet of five airplanes known as the Harper Air Force (after Marian Harper, the Interpublic CEO). The fleet, which included a DC-7 for the boss, was furnished in French provincial. Harper's flying suite boasted a king-size bed, a private library, and a sunken bath. Harper was unrepentant about this luxury. "We can't support people with little thoughts or little dreams," he said (Fox, 1984, p. 266).

During the commission era, agencies used the high remuneration from commissions to "staff up" their work rather than earn super-high profits. They assigned multiple creative teams[5] to creative briefs[6], which permitted agencies to develop a generous number of creative ideas for client consideration. This required highly-staffed creative departments with a mix of senior and junior people. Additionally, agencies maintained high headcounts in the client service (or account management) department, keeping on the payroll at least 1.5 to 2.0 client service people for every creative person in the agency. The client service people were charged with the responsibility to sell the creative ideas to the client, and to manage the relationship to assure continuity and provide high levels of service. Furthermore, client service people were "media salesmen" on behalf of the agency, encouraging clients to spend more aggressively on media. This made great sense, because the more the client spent on media, the more the agency earned through its 15% media commission. A large investment in client service people kept the financial gears of the agency well-oiled.

Writing in 1948 on the financial management of the advertising agency, accountant Ira W. Rubel advised agencies to seek a 20% margin, with "direct expenses" (client serving people costs) at 55% of income and "indirect expenses" (overhead costs) at 25% (Rubel, 1948, p. 121). This would suggest a high ratio of direct-to-indirect costs of 2.2x – a much higher proportion of direct costs than exists today, where the ratio of direct-to-indirect is closer to 1:1x.

The commission edifice began to tumble in 1960, when Shell decided to change both its agency and its form of compensation. Shell announced that it was replacing J Walter Thompson with Ogilvy, Benson & Mather, but the real drama was the new way Shell was going to pay Ogilvy. At Shell's insistence, Ogilvy would work for a fee instead of the usual 15% commission. The fee amounted to the actual cost of operating the account, based on salaries and other cost-accounting variables, plus 25%. This formula would give the agency a 20% profit margin.

Many years later, David Ogilvy took credit for this new fee system, outlining its four advantages, as he saw them:

1. The advertiser pays for the services he wants – no more, no less.

2. Every fee account pays its own way. Unprofitable accounts do not ride on the coat-tails of profitable accounts, which is the case with the commission system.

3. Temporary cuts in clients' [media] budgets do not oblige you to cut staff.

4. When you advise a client to increase his advertising, he does not suspect your motive.

(Ogilvy, 1983, p. 55).

During subsequent years, other Ogilvy clients, including Sears, KLM, American Express and IBM adopted fee arrangements. To the advocates of fees, the method put the agency-client relationship on a more professional basis, like that of attorney or physician, instead of depending on agency salesmanship to persuade the client to spend more on media. *The commission system is an anachronism,"* Ogilvy proudly declared (Fox, 1984, p. 260).

There were compelling economic reasons for changing to fees from commissions. Advertising was a "hot" industry in the 1960s, and media space and time were in short supply. The insatiable demand for advertising drove up media prices at double the rate of GDP inflation – a phenomenon that lasted until the late 1980s, when cable television began to add significant advertising capacity in media. Until then, though, agencies rode the price curve up, earning more and more as their commission income rose proportionately with the rise in media prices. Jay McNamara, a former president of agencies Young & Rubicam and McCann-Erickson Worldwide, looked back on the industry from the vantage point of 1990 and characterized media price inflation as one of the *three key drivers of agency revenue growth* (McNamara, 1990, p. 99).

Advertisers, in contrast to agencies, suffered, having to dig deeper into their pockets every year to pay for increased media costs.

Consequently, beginning in 1960 and continuing thereafter through the 1990s, clients began to experiment with fee-based systems, whereby agencies were paid essentially *by the head* for the people who worked on the clients' accounts. This system paid for the relevant proportion of agencies' client service, strategic planning, creative and production people. Clients paid a proportionate share of the salaries and benefits of these people, in proportion to the time they were expected to allocate to the client, plus an additional mark-up for overhead and profit. Agencies and their clients negotiated the number and seniority of these people, since the agency staff plan was the principal driver of agency fees.

Fee-based remuneration was seen as the solution to the price-inflation problem. The desire to shift to fee-based systems developed a head of steam during the period of media price inflation, and by the next decade, after 2000, the commission system was essentially dead, as nearly all advertisers had converted agency remuneration from commissions to fees.

The commission system had been a rigid, industry-wide 15% fact of life. The shift to fees broke the commission-based price monopoly, and although the shift took decades to accomplish, once it was done it gave advertisers flexibility to exercise new pricing powers – they were now in a position to negotiate fees on an individual agency-by-agency basis. Remuneration became a private and individual affair between client and agency rather than a broad industry convention.

CHAPTER 2 –
THE GOLDEN AGE

"Promise me you'll keep the buzz alive."

The charmed period of advertising was 1945-1975. I call it The Golden Age. It was golden in the sense that headline agencies during this period participated in its growth and profitability; creatives saw their creative reputations enhanced, and commercial activities turned over vast sums of money. This period established the ad agencies' template for success, defining what advertising was (or could be), how relationships ought to be conducted, and what the internal culture of the agency needed to be to assure commercial and creative success.

It may be conventional wisdom that we learn from our failures, but history shows that companies continue to emulate and reinforce what made them successful in the past, even if their marketplaces change beneath them in fundamental and life-threatening ways. (For an in-depth analysis of this, see Clayton M Christensen's classic *The Innovator's Dilemma* (Christensen, 1997)).

Pay close attention to the legacy of The Golden Age, 1945 to 1975, because today's agency cultures are built on the factors that were perceived to have created success during that wonderful era.

Television was a fresh technology after World War II, and the television media owners – the television networks and the local station owners – had plenty of advertising time to sell to potential advertisers. Over time, the demand for television advertising proved to be insatiable, adding to but not replacing radio advertising. TV media owners sold their available advertising time, and excess demand drove up media prices. TV media owners got very, very rich. So did the advertising agencies that created the advertising content, filling the advertising pipeline with innovative and creative work, earning commissions from the growing stream of income that flowed to media owners.

The post-war period created a perfect alignment of factors for the creation of wealth:

1. the population was growing, fueled by the post-war baby boom
2. there was an insatiable post-war demand for products and services, well above the growth of the population, plus
3. banks and tax policies made credit available and desirable, permitting the demand to be financed.

The US growth statistics for this period are extraordinary:

"Between 1950 and 1973 the US population increased by 38%, while disposable personal income increased by 327%. New housing starts went up by 47%, energy

consumption by 121%, college enrollments by 136%, automobile registrations by 151%, telephones in use by 221%, number of outboard motors sold by 242%, retail sales by 250%, families owning two or more cars by 300%, frozen food production by 655%, number of airline passengers by 963%, homes with dishwashers by 1,043%, while homes with room air conditioners rose by 3,662%" (Kleppner, 1979).

During this time, television ruled the marketplace. Households with televisions increased from 9% of all households in 1950 to 87% in 1960 and 97% by 1975, and television drove product sales with print and radio playing supporting roles (Mierau, 2000). The media choice for advertisers was a simple one – TV, print and radio, in that order – and advertisers were ready and willing to pay high prices for the media, in that order. Advertising expenditures rose from $5,780 million in 1950 to $28,320 million in 1975 – a growth of 490%.

Historian Stephen Fox observed the growing influence of TV:

"Though TV still accounted for only about one fourth of gross advertising expenditures, that flickering screen in a box now controlled the ad industry, commanding the best and priciest talent in the business and dominating discussions of the most inventive, effective commercials" (Fox, 1984).

Television was the most expensive medium for advertisers, so the agencies loved it because it made the most money for them – the 15% media commission saw to that. Furthermore, TV ads required the same kind of creativity as Hollywood, so it brought out the closet Hollywood fantasies of the Madison Avenue crowd. Furthermore, TV ads were perceived to be more effective than other types of advertising. TV worked! And because it worked, advertisers fell over themselves buying more and more TV time, encouraged by their advertising agencies. Writing in 1959, author Martin Mayer gushed about the power of television:

"Television is undoubtedly the greatest-selling medium ever devised, for those relatively few advertisers whose market is so large that they do not waste most of television's enormous audience and whose advertising budget is big enough to carry television's enormous costs. The combination of the moving picture and

the speaking voice, both in the consumer's own living room, gives the television advertiser something that is almost the equivalent of a door-to-door sales staff – which makes its visits at a cost considerably less than one cent per call. When the personality presenting the sales pitch is himself a great salesman–an [Arthur] Godfrey, a Steve Allen, a Tennessee Ernie Ford–the advertiser's cup runneth over"(Mayer, 1959).

The agency's client service people assured that their clients understood the message about television's effectiveness. Client service people were, in reality, salesmen for the concept of TV advertising, convincing their clients to spend big on television and to buy ever-growing amounts of national advertising time. The message rarely failed. As long as their clients bought TV advertising, the agency's 15% commissions guaranteed a positive inflow of cash, enough to cover all the work and all the costs of the agency, with plenty left over for profits.

This was one of the beauties of the commission system. The agency sold the client on the effectiveness of TV rather than on the special capabilities of the agency. It could be shown that advertisers who out-spent their competitors on a consistent basis gained market share, and the advertisers who dominated category spend – companies like Proctor & Gamble in detergents, for example – protected their leading market share positions. *"If you want to be as dominant as P&G, agencies would say, you have to spend like P&G – outspend your competitors, year after year, in good times and in bad times."* It was hard to argue with the logic. The television research data, established by AC Nielsen in 1950, proved the case.

Client service people didn't just talk about agency capabilities – they *showed* agency capabilities on a daily basis. They provided unlimited service and brought a steady stream of clever creative ideas for approval. This was easy and fun, even if it was deadline-intensive. It required very little in the way of genuine management expertise. As long as there was 15% commission income, an agency could afford great creative talent and give the client as much service as it needed: sales meeting materials, management presentations (to make client executives look good), competitive reviews, restaurant bookings, sports tickets – anything was possible. Unlimited service bought good will up and down the client's organization, and this made the ground fertile for the hard sell on increased TV advertising.

Fee negotiations, too, were relatively simple during The Golden Age. The agency did not have to put forward a proposal for agency compensation, justifying how many people worked on the account or what they did. Compensation was worked out by how much money the client was prepared to spend on media.

A senior ad agency executive would get the client's CEO and chief marketing officer (CMO) excited about a high level of next year's media spend – and the market share increases that might be expected – and once this was done the client service organization could be turned loose on the rest of the client's marketing organization, lining them up to expect and desire a big year with big advertising budgets. Once the media budgets were agreed and approved, the agency had to deliver the goods: provide unlimited service, create and deliver great ideas and produce terrific ads. It was hoped that the clients' products would sell well in the marketplace. This was easier said than done. If a client's sales fell short of expectations, then media budgets would be cut, usually in the 4th quarter, to make up for any product sales or profit shortfalls. This would certainly affect agency income for the year. It was important, then, for agencies to convince their clients that media expenditures be viewed as sacred and untouchable, whatever the circumstances, in good sales years as well as bad, rather than as spigots to be turned down or off in a reactionary manner.

This is why agencies' client service teams worked so hard to influence the thinking about media spend at every level in clients' organization. Agencies staffed their accounts to provide "cover" at every hierarchical level, from the lowly brand managers at the bottom to the chairman and chief executive at the top. This took a large number of client service people – from 1.5 to 2 client service people for every creative who worked on the account.

Service was not exclusively a client service responsibility during The Golden Age. Creatives had a role to play, as well. The head of the creative department would assign multiple creative teams to work on client briefs – in effect, assigning extra creatives to the work – so that the agency could generate a *surplus* of creative ideas. The idea behind this was simple. *Take ten ideas to the client rather than three. Give the client a choice. Show the client how creative the agency can be. Exceed their expectations. Some ideas will be rejected, to be sure. Others will "stick." Rework the positive material until you get it right and get the client to give approval for production. Help the client feel good about spending so much on media. Over-deliver!*

Global advertising network BBDO highlighted this work ethic via their well-known motto: "*The work, the work, the work,*" featuring its creative work prominently in its communications to clients and potential clients.

"Work" really meant "work it until you've generated the slam-bang big idea" for the brand – the kind of idea that generates brand successes and makes the client want to spend even more on media.

In the vocabulary of 2015, these "big ideas" are "taglines," and they're meant to sum up a brand's meaning in an enduring way. Past and present taglines include McDonalds': *I'm Lovin' It.* Budweiser: *The King of Beers.* Nike: *Just Do It.* Kentucky Fried Chicken: *Finger Lickin' Good.* De Beers: *A Diamond is Forever.* You get the idea – you've been bombarded with taglines your entire life.

David Ogilvy, founder of Ogilvy & Mather, described the "big idea" concept in 1983:

> "**What's the big idea?** *You can do homework from now until domesday, but you will never win fame and fortune unless you also invent big ideas. It takes a big idea to attract the attention of consumers and get them to buy your product. Unless your advertising contains a big idea, it will pass like a ship in the night. I doubt if more than one campaign in a hundred contains a big idea. I am supposed to be one of the more fertile inventors of big ideas, but in my long career as a copywriter I have not had more than 20, if that. Big ideas come from the unconscious...But your unconscious has to be well informed, or your idea will be irrelevant. Stuff your conscious mind with information, then unhook your ratio-*

nal thought process. You can help this process by going for a long walk, or taking a hot bath, or drinking half a pint of claret"

(Ogilvy, 1983, p. 16).

Big ideas are generated by creative teams. Creative teams consist of an art director and a copywriter – an images/sounds person and a words person – who work closely together, often for years, bouncing concepts back and forth to one another, feeding on each other's capabilities, functioning as a self-contained ideas machine within the creative heart of the agency.

The industry had been in the creative doldrums in the years immediately after World War II. Leo Burnett, founder of the agency that bore his name, long held the opinion that his industry had had "too much dull advertising, pages and pages of dull, stupid, uninteresting copy that does not offer the reader anything in return for his time taken in reading it" (Fox, 1984, p. 221).

He celebrated *creativity* and encouraged his agency and others, as well, to celebrate "the creative men who are the men of the hour. It is high time that they were given the respect that they deserve," he wrote in 1955. He pushed his creatives to find "the inherent drama in the product itself and present it believably, like a news story, using non-verbal archetypes and symbols, often drawn from American history and folklore." Under his leadership, Leo Burnett created the Jolly Green Giant, the Pillsbury Doughboy, Tony the Tiger and the Marlboro Man (Fox, 1984, pp. 221-223).

Separately, Bill Bernbach, the creative founder of Dane Doyle Bernbach, developed innovative 1950s ads for Volkswagen (*Think Small*) and Avis (*We're No. 2; We Try Harder*), while David Ogilvy invented *The Hathaway Man* in 1951 for Hathaway Shirts.

The industry coined the phrase "The Creative Revolution" for the change from dull advertising to the whimsical Big Ideas of the 1950s and 1960s.

Jerry Della Femina, head of Della Femina & Partners and well-known creative figure in his own right[7] celebrated these accomplishments in 1970: *"In the beginning, there was Volkswagen. That's the first campaign which everyone can trace back and say, 'This is where the changeover began'. That was the day when the new advertising agency was really born, and it all started with Doyle, Dane, Bernbach. They began as an agency around 1949 and they were known in the business as a good agency, but no one really got to see what they were doing until Volkswagen came around"* (Femina, 1970).

The Volkswagen campaigns turned the industry on its head – this was *creativity writ large*. Every advertiser wanted and sought comparable *Creative Revolution Big Ideas* for their campaigns. *Creativity* sold products! The Creative Revolution kicked off a burst of sustained demand for advertising that increased industry growth, created excess demand that drove up the price of media and lined agency pockets with 15% commissions.

Mary Wells established Wells, Rich, and Greene in 1963 with one $6 million client, and she grew the agency spectacularly to more than $100 million in billings in five years by focusing on Creative Revolution work, including *"I can't believe I ate the whole thing"* for Alka-Seltzer and *the 100-millimeter cigarette* for Benson & Hedges (Fox, 1984, pp. 268-269).

Fifty years later, in his 2011 memoir, John Hegarty, the creative founding partner of Bartle Beatty Hegarty reiterated the Creative Revolution refrain:

> *"Ideas are what advertising is built upon. We worship them, we seek them, fight over them, applaud them and value them above everything else. Walk round the floors of any agency and the phrase you'll most hear is: 'What's the idea?'"* (Hegarty, 2011).

"Big ideas" and "creativity" combined with "unlimited service" defined the formula for agency success. These factors came together during the 15% commission era, during The Golden Age, and they have served as guideposts for agency executives ever since.

The advertising business was financially attractive for agency owners. The 1960s would be remembered not only for the Creative Revolution but also as the decade when advertising agencies went public, rewarding themselves for their successes to date and setting themselves up with strengthened finances for globalization and other initiatives. Papert, Koenig, Lois (PKL) took the plunge in 1962, setting a trend which was initially frowned upon by the industry (Fox, 1984). PKL was followed by Foote, Cone & Belding and DDB in 1964, Grey in 1965, Ogilvy & Mather in 1966 and J Walter Thompson in 1969.

During the first seven months of 1969, attracted by high industry growth and the prospect of wealth, nearly 100 new agencies were launched. Newsweek put the Creative Revolution on its cover in August 1969. Advertising was the place to be for would-be entrepreneurs.

The 30 years of The Golden Age, 1946-1975, was a period of growth and wealth creation. Agencies focused on creativity and service. The commission system provided high levels of income, making the large cost investments affordable. The Golden Age was successful for advertised brands, and what was good for clients created success for agencies. Agency executives hammered home the simple themes of creativity and service, and in doing so they created an enduring theme for agency culture for the decades to come.

CHAPTER 3 – THE HOLDING COMPANIES

"Who is our most creative accountant?"

Credit: William Hamilton / The New Yorker / The Cartoon Bank.

The success of ad agencies during the Creative Revolution attracted financial acquirers and, eventually, as author Mark Tungate observed in his highly readable history of global advertising, *Ad Land* (Tungate, 2007), "almost everyone in advertising works for one of five different companies." Those five companies are, of course, the behemoth holding companies WPP (British), Omnicom Group (American), The Interpublic Group of Companies (American), Publicis Groupe (French), and Dentsu Inc. (Japanese), which together bought up during the past 30 years a significant portion of the world's global advertising agencies, direct marketing agencies, digital and social agencies, market research companies, media agencies and public relations firms.

The holding companies created a dominant ownership position in the industry and created a presence that changed the equilibrium between ad agencies, who focused on creativity and service, and their clients, who wanted from the agencies whatever "worked." The new imperative brought by the holding companies required agencies to generate higher and growing profit margins, year after year. Early in the holding company/agency relationships, when agencies were well paid and "fat" with resources, this new imperative did not pose problems – agencies could easily cut costs to improve their profits. This caused no damage to their operations or their ability to service clients. Later, when industry conditions deteriorated with lower fees and greater workloads, the profit generation imperative would begin to stretch if not cripple agency capabilities.

Each holding company came into existence for different reasons, as discussed below. In chronological order, here is a brief sketch of early holding company histories:

> **Interpublic.** The Interpublic Group of Companies was the grandfather of them all, born in 1960 as the handiwork of McCann-Erickson's merger-obsessed President, Marion Harper, Junior, who rose from the mailroom at age 23 to become president of the agency by age 32. Harper had grand ambitions, and he was bent on leaping to dominance in the industry through account wins and acquisitions of other agencies. Marschalk & Pratt, an acquired agency, was maintained as a separate entity with its own office and identity. Further agencies were acquired, and in 1960, Harper announced a rescrambling of the ensemble into a new conglomerate, Interpublic, with four initial divisions: McCann-Erickson, to handle domestic accounts; McCann-Marschalk, a second "traditional" agency, to handle competing accounts; McCann-Erickson Corp. (International), to handle nearly 50 overseas offices; and Communications Affiliates, offering various research, public relations, and sales promotion services (Fox, 1984, pp. 198-199).

> Interpublic's marquee advertising agencies today include Deutsch, FCB, The Martin Agency, McCann and RG/A.

47

WPP. Next in line some 25 years later was a pure holding company start-up, WPP, begun by Martin Sorrell (Sir Martin from 2000 onwards) and stockbroker Preston Rabl, who raised a loan to acquire Wire & Plastic Products, a manufacturer of shopping baskets, to serve as a shell company for a straightforward program of ad agency acquisitions. Sorrell, a Harvard Business School graduate with an MBA, had worked at Saatchi & Saatchi since 1975, and after 1977 he had been their group finance director. He learned the acquisitions business thoroughly. During his stewardship, Saatchi & Saatchi completed more than 15 agency acquisitions in the UK, US and elsewhere in the world, using Saatchi & Saatchi stock, debt and "earn-out" structures that motivated agency owners / managers to improve their financial performance as a way of earning a higher final price for their companies.

In June 1987, Sorrell borrowed heavily and WPP completed the industry's first hostile takeover, acquiring JWT for US $566 million. Subsequently, in 1989, Sorrell pursued and won Ogilvy & Mather for $860 million, using debt and preferred stock rather than equity. By 2000, he secured Young & Rubicam for US $4.7 billion, and in 2005, Grey Global Group for US $1.75 billion (Tungate, 2007, pp. 164-165). Along the way, WPP completed many other acquisitions in various media, and Sorrell consolidated the media departments of his various holdings into GroupM, a media powerhouse. Later, WPP pursued an aggressive program of digital agency acquisitions and by 2013 had 150 major holdings in advertising, media, research, public relations, branding, healthcare, direct marketing, digital, promotion, and specialist communications (Annual Report, 2013).

Major ad agency brands today include Grey, JWT, O&M and Y&R.

Omnicom. Concurrently in 1986, but along very different lines, Keith Reinhard of Needham Harper sought to pair his agency with the highly regarded BBDO and DDB agencies, seeking scale in an industry that was then highly fragmented. The three agencies eventually came together as Omnicom, a mega-agency that segued into a three-legged structure involving two surviving (and competing) agencies, BBDO and DDB Needham (a merger of DDB and Needham Harper), and a third entity called Diversified Agency Group, which gathered together the assorted direct marketing, public relations and sales promotion activities of the member agencies.

The press nicknamed the deal "The Big Bang" (Tungate, 2007, p. 166). Allen G Rosenshine, Chairman and CEO of BBDO called the new agency entity "nothing less than advertising's global creative superpower," capable of providing extra creative resources for clients, providing a structure that could hold on to restless creative talent, and introducing a higher-level organization to handle new business pitches. Ed Meyer, chairman of Grey Advertising, a competitor, was skeptical of these claims. "This is their own version of the Interpublic Group of Companies. I don't understand why Doyle Dane and Needham felt that they had to add BBDO – they seem to be big enough" (Dougherty, 1986).

Omnicom's major ad agencies today include BBDO, DDB and TBWA.

Publicis Groupe. Publicis, the French advertising agency founded by the innovative Marcel Bleustein-Blanchet in 1926, went public in 1970 and expanded along European lines until 1988, when under its Chairman and CEO Maurice Lévy it entered into an alliance with FCB. Publicis-FCB became the largest European network with one worldwide footprint via Publicis' 40 agencies in Europe and the US and FCB's 176 agencies located in 40 countries. However, when FCB's Chief Executive Norman Brown retired and was replaced by Bruce Mason, Mason was not favorable to the alliance, and in 1996 it was dissolved. To make up for lost time, Lévy set off on an acquisition trail, buying Hal Riney & Partners, Fallon McElligott and, in 2000, the fabled Saatchi & Saatchi. Subsequently, in 2002, Lévy negotiated a merger with Bcom3, the temporary holding company for Leo Burnett and the MacManus Group (D'Arcy Masius Benton & Bowles, along with N.W. Ayer and Partners) (Tungate, 2007, pp. 176-179).

Subsequent acquisitions were designed to turn the holding company into a digital giant: Digitas (USA), Business Interactif (France), CCG (China), Tribal (Brazil), Phonevalley, Performics and Razorfish, purchased from Microsoft Corporation.

In 2013, Publicis and Omnicom announced that they would merge "as equals" and become the #1 holding company in size, but much to the embarrassment of both parties, they were unable to pull off the deal in 2014 as a result of tax complications and disagreements over who would be the finance director, a Frenchman or an American. After the failure of this deal, Publicis bought Sapient, a digital technology provider with digital advertising interests, for $3.7 billion.

Publicis' major traditional ad agencies include BBH, Fallon, Leo Burnett, Publicis Worldwide and Saatchi & Saatchi.

Dentsu. Dentsu had long been the world's largest advertising and media *agency*, operating from a dominant position in Japan and having strategic Dentsu outposts throughout South East Asia and elsewhere. In recent years, particularly since 2007, Dentsu made a number of focused acquisitions of limited scale – the US creative hotshops Attik (2007) and mcgarrybowen (2008); the US digital firms 360i (2010), Ignition One (2010)[8], Netmining (2010), Firstborn (2011) and Steak (2011); the PR group Mitchell Communications (2013), and in India Taproot (2012) and Webchutney (2013). Then, in 2013, Dentsu upped the ante through a $5 billion acquisition of London-based media company Aegis, owner of Carat, iProspect, Isobar, Posterscope, Vizeum and Aztec, putting Dentsu in the number five position in the industry with income of $6.4 billion (Adage Data Center, 2013). Consistent with its increased globalization and geographical reach, Dentsu upgraded its management structure, anointing Jerry Buhlman, CEO of the Aegis Network, as a Dentsu executive officer in June 2013 – joining his boss, Tim Andree (director and executive VP of Dentsu Inc.) as the second of only two non-Japanese to be named executive officers (Dentsu Taps Aegis Executive, 2013).

Major agency brands today include Dentsu and mcgarrybowen.

Despite the differences in formation history and acquisition strategies, each holding company began to resemble its competitors, developing common goals and concerns that affected the operations of their respective portfolios of ad agencies. There were four major holding company management priorities:

1. **Improve the financial performance of portfolio companies**. Each holding company demanded improved profit performance out of each of its owned agencies. This was not a one-time request to be accomplished after an agency was acquired; instead, it was a major ongoing activity that dominated the relationship between the holding company and its owned agencies, from budget setting time (typically during October-December for the following fiscal year) through quarterly reviews and end-of-year closings.

   Like any owner of a diversified portfolio, the holding company established profit margin goals for each agency, and these goals were documented in the agreed agency budget with specific revenue and cost targets by client, region and office. It goes without saying that these holding company profit goals were "stretch" goals, and that the "stretch" became harder to achieve in the face of ongoing client fee reductions. The typical holding company came to expect a 15-20% operating margin from its operating companies.

   One common metric used by holding companies to evaluate agency operations was "staff-cost ratio," or the cost of all agency personnel divided by agency income. Staff-cost ratio took the total of staff costs and divided them by income, yielding a "ratio" or "percentage." The holding company would set a "benchmark," like 50%, for the staff-cost ratio, on the assumption that this would optimize agency operations and deliver an appropriate profit margin. If an agency had a higher ratio of (say) 55%, meaning that staff costs were 55% of agency income, then the agency was deemed to be "high cost," and agency management was expected to cut agency staff costs accordingly. The alternative interpretation, that the agency was "low income" rather than "high cost" was not considered.

This metric was effective during the decade of the 1990s and shortly thereafter, when agency remuneration was high and agencies were staffing their clients heavily with multiple creative teams and a full complement of client service people. However, as agency income eroded, and declining income mathematically drove up staff-cost ratios (the denominator was declining, so the ratio rose), agencies were still expected to reduce costs and get the ratio in line. It did not matter if workloads were growing and more staff was required; the staff-cost ratio dictated a lower agency headcount and cost structure. Agencies did their very best to meet holding company staff-cost ratio targets.

2. **Use purchasing leverage to negotiate lower costs with key suppliers.** The holding company's purchasing scale was an obvious source of lower-cost value-added for individual agencies. Prices of hotels, airline travel, telecommunications costs, IT costs, stationery/paper supplies and like items were negotiated effectively by procurement executives at the holding company to give their agencies lower costs in key parts of their cost structures.

3. **Seek to grow organic top-line revenue.** Apart from encouraging revenue growth from the individual agencies, holding companies acted independently, selling the concept of "holding company relationships" to large global advertisers. In this type of scheme, clients agreed to use principally, or wholly, the agencies owned by the holding company. In return for this exclusivity, and on the assumption that there were genuine economies of scale from holding company relationships (a debatable claim), the holding companies offered a fee discount of some type. Needless to say, many of their agencies saw the promotion of holding company relationships as directly competitive with agencies' new business marketing activities, with the holding company "brand" eclipsing ad agency brands. As one senior agency executive explained to me, "it's one thing for us to go out there and win a new client. It's another thing to be a cog in the wheel of a low-priced holding company relationship. I've appreciated the revenue that it brings us, but I'm concerned about damage to our agency's brand name."

4. **Grow holding company size through further acquisitions**. All the holding companies developed considerable acquisitions experience, not only in negotiating terms of acquisitions but in integrating acquired agencies into the holding company's portfolio. New or upgraded budgeting, financial and reporting systems had to be put in place, and the holding company's budgetary and cost controls implemented immediately. Holding companies were aggressive acquirers of marketing services companies around the world, not only in digital and social technologies, but also in strong-growth markets, like Brazil, Russia, India and China (the BRIC countries). Hardly a week could go by without the announcement of new holding company acquisitions in one part of the world or another.

The consolidation of holding company power and position in the industry is one of the fascinating aspects of advertising industry change since the 1980s. Industry spokesmen evolved from agency CEOs (i.e., David Ogilvy, Leo Burnett, etc.) and famous creatives (Bill Bernbach, Jay Chiat, Lee Clow, Hal Riney, and so on) to holding company CEOs (Sir Martin Sorrell and Maurice Lévy). Freewheeling and undisciplined agency spending on people, parties and creative pitches were replaced by sober agency consideration of salary levels, headcounts, overhead rates and profit margins. Holding companies brought discipline and profit consciousness to the creative free-for-all that had been the trademark of ad agencies during The Golden Age. Holding companies did not kill all the fun, to be sure, but their involvement was like that of a sober spouse at a cocktail party, reminding you of tomorrow's hangover if you indulge too much.

CHAPTER 4 –
MIXED OUTCOMES
1973-1990

"These are our golden oldies."

Credit: Joseph Farris / The New Yorker / The Cartoon Bank.

Global events beginning in 1973 led to major hurdles in the post-World War II economic boom, and they were followed by a number of changes in the advertising business that had long-lasting consequences. However, from 1973 through to 1990, ad agencies continued their successful and astonishing financial performance, riding a wave of inflated media prices and earning media commissions along the way. Agency revenues and profits continued to rise even though the major economies of the world were having difficulties and advertisers, themselves, were struggling:

"...billings at the top agencies and total advertising expenditures increased faster than the GNP, even faster than inflation or any other economic indicator. In a time of generally stuttering economic growth, advertising enjoyed remarkable, almost giddy leaps forward. Total spending on advertising grew from $19.6 billion in 1970 to $54.6 billion in 1980; TV as usual led the way, from $3.6 billion to $11.4 billion. In 1970 world billings [were] $773 million for J Walter Thompson, the leading agency. Ten years later, thirteen agencies [were] billion-dollar operations" (Fox, 1984, p. 327).

OAPEC and the first oil shock. In October 1973, the Organization of Arab Petroleum Exporting Countries (OAPEC) announced an embargo against countries that supported Israel in the Yom Kippur War against Syria and Egypt. The embargo was lifted in 1974, but it was followed by an upsurge in oil prices as OAPEC began to use its leverage by raising world oil prices.

This first oil shock raised energy costs for corporations. Prices rose for all products, particularly those with high-energy content (steel, aluminum, and so on) or made from materials based on petrochemicals, such as plastics. Prices could not be raised enough to cover cost increases, so all-important corporate earnings were threatened. Executives responded in a number of ways, particularly by creating energy task forces to identify energy usage in their manufacturing and distribution operations and by developing conservation measures to cut costs.

The 1974 energy task forces, out on the hunt for energy cost savings, established an early precedent for what would later become, for different reasons, procurement-led hunts for cost savings within marketing departments and from marketing suppliers like ad agencies.

High prices, driven by higher energy costs, and high unemployment from the associated recession took the growth out of consumer markets. In addition, traditional industries like steel-making and automobile manufacturing suffered as newly industrialized countries stepped up the competition through low-cost exports. The Stock Market crashed in 1973-74 and the associated pain was felt until the spring of 1975. In the UK, the oil crisis was compounded by the imposition of a three-day week amid fears of power shortages following the announcement of a coal miners' strike. There were widespread power blackouts across the country. UK inflation peaked at 20%.

Recovery, then 1980-82 recessions. Economies began to grow in late 1975, along with inflation, but in 1980, followed by 1981-82, a severe double-dip recession resulted from a variety of factors. One of these factors was another energy crisis, this time created by the Iranian Revolution of 1979 and the subsequent interruption in the smooth flow of oil from the producing countries to the oil-consuming world. This second oil shock initiated a second round of energy cost investigations in the corporate world and helped to institutionalize what later became permanent cost reduction initiatives in major corporations.

Media Inflation Cushion 1975-1990. Advertising agencies were relatively insulated from these adverse economic factors, since media price inflation provided a revenue and profit cushion during the 1970s and 1980s. Media airtime remained in short supply, and the excess of media demand over media supply drove up media prices and the agency commission income that was tied to them. As welcome as this was for agency executives, it was probably not in their best long-term interests, since their hard-pressed clients were footing the bill during the difficult times of the 1970s and 1980s, and resentments were building up. Agencies looked fat and arrogant at a time when their clients were making sacrifices.

Visible agency wealth. Strong financial performance encouraged ad agencies to go public, and public ownership took certain agencies on the acquisition trail, providing a degree of visibility about agency richness that was both embarrassing and irritating. "At the center of it all was Saatchi & Saatchi," remarked journalist and author Mark Tungate (Tungate, 2007). Saatchi & Saatchi went public in 1976. By 1987 Saatchi & Saatchi PLC had acquired more than 35 marketing services businesses, including four significant ad agency networks (Goldman, 1997). Tungate put the total price tag of these acquisitions at over US $1 billion, and with a minimum of organic growth Saatchi & Saatchi PLC expanded to 18,000 employees in 500 offices across 65 countries (Tungate, 2007, p. 101).

Saatchi & Saatchi's 1986 acquisition of the privately held Ted Bates Worldwide agency had industry-wide reverberations. The price, more than $500 million, was five times larger than any previously paid for an advertising firm. The deal gained Bob Jacoby, the Ted Bates CEO, a personal fortune of $111 million and turned 100 other Bates employees into instant millionaires. The transaction also turned Jacoby into the industry's most prominent outcast. "A living symbol of greed," Tom Delaney, [then] a senior editor for the trade journal Adweek, put it (Kleiner, 1987).

Nearly 30 years later, advertising people still remember the Jacoby affair. Writing in Forbes.com in 2012, Avi Dan, who was an account director at Benton & Bowles in the 1980s, recalled the shock:

> *"Marketers were flabbergasted. They did not realize that their agency partners were able to monetize their relationships for so much money. Clearly, they concluded, agency profits were much higher than the agencies were letting on.*
>
> *They quickly decided that it was now time for reassessing how agencies are compensated. Heretofore, agencies were collecting a commission of 15% on the media they placed for marketers. With media inflation rising on average 10% every year as far back as the eye can see, the agencies doubled their profits every seven years.*
>
> *Once marketers realized that the commission system favored the agencies disproportionately and unfairly, they started switching to a more equitable compensation system" (Dan, June 21, 2012).*

Internal cultural shifts. Public ownership (and later, holding company ownership) brought about internal cultural shifts that many executives later regretted. Increased public or holding company ownership was marked by "a shift from the creative departments to management, from little boutiques to bigness and mergers, from vivid personalities to corporate anonymity," according to historian Stephen Fox (Fox, 1984, p. 314). "In retrospect," George Lois said of his experience both pre- and post-public ownership at Papert, Koenig, Lois (which went public in 1962 and shut down after client and management losses in 1969) "public ownership was the catalyst for destroying our

57

partnership. People became rich quick and choked up. They started to think, 'We now have obligations to our stockholders'" (Fox, 1984, p. 317).

J Walter Thompson, Foote, Cone & Belding, DDB, Grey and Ogilvy & Mather were all public companies by 1969, and the need to focus on profits was top of mind. This focus would intensify in later years when each was merged into or was acquired by one of the holding companies.

Globalization. Globalization added an additional complexity for large agencies, as their global clients reorganized to produce and sell homogeneous, high-quality, low-priced products throughout the world. "Success in world competition," wrote Theodore Levitt of Harvard Business School in a landmark *Harvard Business Review* article in 1983, "turns on efficiency in production, distribution, marketing, and management, and inevitably becomes focused on price. The world's needs and desires have been irrevocably homogenized" (Levitt, 1983). Levitt's emphasis on globalization made him one of Maurice Saatchi's favorite mentors, and Levitt was eventually appointed to Saatchi & Saatchi's board of directors.

Globalization turned traditional marketing on its head. No longer could companies treat the local consumer as king, serving him/her with locally produced advertising for customized products and services that met local preferences. Instead, according to Levitt, "the global competitor [must] seek constantly to standardize its offering everywhere...customers will prefer its world-standardized products."

Globalization struck at the heart of local agency office operations and began a process of agency reorganization. Previously, local agency offices around the world created local ads for their local advertiser clients – like Grey Germany working for P&G Germany, for example. Grey Germany addressed the needs of German P&G customers, using the full capabilities of agency people in Grey's German office – and earned local media commissions from the airing and printing of ads in German markets. The New York, London, Paris, Dusseldorf, Madrid and Milan offices of a global agency like Grey might have the same name on the door and serve the same global client – but they operated as six independent entities, dealing with their US, UK, French, German, Spanish and Italian clients in independent ways.

Globalization changed this structure. Instead of producing six different ads for a consumer product, globalization encouraged *the homogenization of ads*, much in the same way that the client's products were homogenized for sale in global markets. In fact, globalization required the homogenization of ads, so that the brand message could be uniform and consistent, completely aligned with the product, around the globe.

Globalization led to the *centralization of ad creation*, typically in New York or London, with Paris, Dusseldorf, Madrid and Milan (and many other offices) *adapting* centrally produced ads for local consumption. A genuine adaptation would require very little new creative time from the local market and very few client service resources to get the ad through the local client's approval process. Consequently, a global policy of centralized ad creation with local ad adaptation was a lower-cost strategy in total, and it certainly involved lower costs in the local office.

Clients figured this out quickly, and as globalization practices were put in place around the world, clients considered changes in agency remuneration plans. Instead of paying agencies on a 15% commission basis, global clients reasoned that since globalization was reducing agency headcounts, agency remuneration should be reduced as well. By 1990, clients began cutting the standard 15% commission to as low as 11%, and a majority of agencies went along (Goldman, 1997, p. 107). Later, commissions would give way to labor-based fees. This shift in remuneration took years to work its way through the list of big-spending advertisers, but the logic was established early in the globalization game, adding another source of downwards pressure on agency remuneration.

Agencies found themselves ill-equipped to deal with globalization. Local offices, fighting to maintain their size and income, resisted globalization efforts and conspired with their local clients to thwart the takeover of marketing by the global guys. Their local clients, too, learned that they had much at stake. If globalization was a success, then local marketing organizations had only a limited marketing role to play. Local agencies and local clients dug in their heels and resisted global efforts. They complained that centrally-created ads missed the mark in their unique local markets. Globalization surfaced new conflicts between local operations and headquarters operations. In the meantime, the executives at the center of the storm – at advertiser or agency headquarters – scratched their heads and fumed over the organizational resistance. They were relatively powerless to dictate terms to their regions, but they could not stand back and watch globalization fail.

The requirements of globalization forced agencies to confront the management and operational independence of their local offices. Up to this point, each office operated under an office head as a standalone entity with its own responsibility for income and costs. Office heads were perceived as the real centers of power in the agency network, and they were capable of telling senior executives in the agency center to "stick it" if they felt like it. After all, office heads had their own clients and revenues, and they developed new clients. No one at the agency headquarters really knew what any office head was doing. Traditionally, office heads were left alone to run their shops, and headquarters stayed out.

Globalization, though, cut out the local offices in ways that undermined the stature and power of office heads. In the worst of cases, at least in the eyes of an office head, global client fees came to an office as an *allocation*, a piece of a global pie. The pie was negotiated by a centrally-based finance director, a CEO, a holding company executive or a global client head. The size of *the local piece of pie* was determined in an arbitrary way. Inevitably, local offices felt left out and short-changed by this, and they resented globalization initiatives – they diluted the power and position of local offices, and created a confusing network of ambiguous relationships within the agency. Who was more important – an office head or a global client head? Vocally, office heads complained that globalization hurt their profits. If office profits fell short at the end of a year, office heads pointed the finger at low global client fees as the culprit. Too little money for too much work, they said. And there was nothing they could do about it except grouse and fight territorial battles with global client heads, who were elsewhere in the world, flitting about between their global clients and the network of agency offices, responsible for big visible bucks, leaving the painful aspects of globalization for the local office heads to sort out. It did not matter if global income was high or low; local office heads still had to deliver required profit margins. Globalization made this harder, they said.

Supply chain efficiency. Globalization had other effects, and one of these was to motivate corporations to develop programs that would lower global costs while improving global quality. This went beyond finding the energy cost savings that they sought as a result of the oil shocks. Competitors were global competitors; global companies had to achieve cost positions at least as low as their major global competitors. Economist William Shepherd estimated that industry deregulation, together with anti-trust actions by the government, had served to increase the portion of the US economy "subject to effective competition from 56% in 1958 to 77% by 1980" (Kiechel, 2010, p. 174), so there was some urgency for US corporations to get it right. Remember what Ted Levitt wrote in 1983? *"Success in world competition turns on efficiency in production, distribution, marketing, and management, and inevitably becomes focused on price."* Increasingly, companies who sought these efficiencies went down a predictable path, building on the experience of the energy-reduction efforts, organizing internal task forces and hiring management consultants to carry out wide-ranging studies that examined not only the efficiency of the corporation's own operations *but those of their suppliers as well.*

1. **Global supply chain management**. Global companies shuttered their inefficient internal manufacturing operations and expanded their use of outside lower-cost strategic suppliers, who were expected to design, produce and deliver products and services at low cost with high quality. This required a revolution in the way companies worked with suppliers. A new science of supply chain management sprang into being, along with quality management programs and certification programs like ISO 9001 to guide the transformations. Outside suppliers obtained quality certifications and opened up their operations to make their costs and processes transparent; they worked hard to achieve the rigorous quality and cost standards es-

tablished by their customers. Significantly, they were given a larger role to play in their customers' operations. The list of qualified suppliers was significantly pruned, so that only a handful of suppliers remained on the list of strategic suppliers, and each of them became responsible for significantly larger volumes of design and production. Additionally, strategic suppliers were given design-and-produce responsibilities rather than produce at the lowest cost. Strategic suppliers became an integral part of their customers' operations, engaging in proprietary R&D as well as production design. This tied the fortunes of suppliers with the fortunes of their customers, and vice versa.

2. **Procurement departments**. Global companies empowered their procurement departments (sometimes called strategic sourcing or purchasing) to lead supply chain improvements. Often, procurement brought in outside management consultants to help provide analysis and direction for the supply chain and process review programs. As procurement departments uncovered and eliminated inefficiencies, they grew in corporate power – here was a department that could deliver increased efficiencies and profits on a reliable basis. Incremental dollars invested in procurement activities provided a reliable return – a better return on investment than the speculative dollars invested in marketing, some thought.

3. **Process reviews**. Procurement departments examined and overhauled the processes that generated costs, inefficiencies and waste – and sought to eliminate all non-value-added activities, which were believed to add up to more than 30% of value-added costs. In the 1990s, this concept was popularized as business process reengineering (BPR) by Michael Hammer and James Champy in their *Reengineering the Corporation: A Manifesto for Business Revolution* (Hammer & Champy, 1993). The process to uncover process inefficiencies cut across all departments and all organizational structures in a corporation. The process became a horizontal cost hunt across vertically organized corporations, facilitating an inspection of previously protected domains, and it empowered procurement departments with their operational specialists and analysts at the expense of previously untouchable silos, like manufacturing and marketing. Indeed, BPR activities threw

the organizational chart out the window. Although the traditional organizational chart continued to show vertical management structures, the actual power structure was as much horizontal as vertical. As Hammer and Champy described it, *"Once it is restructured, process teams – groups of people working together to perform an entire process – turn out to be the logical way to organize the people who perform the work. Process teams don't contain representatives from all the functional departments involved. Rather, process teams replace the old departmental structure."* (Hammer & Champy, 1993, p. 70).

When BPR investigations later migrated to analyze media and advertising costs, agencies and their fees became more broadly exposed to procurement's analyses, and chief marketing officers were no longer in a position to protect their favored agencies. Marketing began to lose control over what happened to its ad agencies. Procurement entered the picture in a big way and soon would be the driving force for the determination of ad agency fees. Marketing was reluctant to intervene; they had their own problems justifying their own cost structures. Agencies would have to sort out procurement on their own.

CHAPTER 5 –
SHAREHOLDER VALUE:
1990 AND ONWARDS

"It was at this point, gentlemen, that reality intruded."

A d agencies had their hands full after 1990. There was another belt-tightening recession, this time in 1990-91, and the recession added to an already existing slow-down in advertising expenditures, particularly in the US (Goldman, 1997, p. 107). An expansion of cable television capacity was putting an end to the media shortage that led to media price inflation. Commission rates were on the decline and fee-based compensation was replacing commission-based income in any case.

One accelerating factor for the shift to fee-based remuneration was the strategic spin-off of media buying and selling operations from full-service ad agencies, leading to the formation of standalone media agencies that left behind the creative service parts of their previous agencies.[9] Full-service agencies had been spinning off their media planning and buying capabilities so their media operations could compete more successfully against stand-alone media agencies like Carat and CIA, which were picking up the media needs of advertisers through aggressive selling and pricing. Stand-alone media agencies operated on commissions in the range of 4-5%. This left a 10-11% commission from the original 15% commission for the residual creative services agencies, but the justification for a media commission of any magnitude for creative agencies was a weak one. Advertisers used this argument as a basis for shifting creative agency remuneration from commission-based to fee-based arrangements.

Procurement departments were flexing their muscles, and media costs and agency fees were starting to come under their scrutiny. The early fee and commission cuts that resulted from this process were modest, and they were small cuts relative to the high levels of remuneration that were being paid, so the pain was negligible. Nevertheless, the agency remuneration pattern was set – the direction was clearly downwards.

Separately, clients were globalizing, and agencies were doing their best to respond, but the fragmented agency organizational structure was a difficult one to tame, and resistance to global initiatives was very real and highly frustrating. Agencies were new at this globalization game, and it would take time and sophistication to figure out how to manage the decentralized agency network structure.

JWT and Ogilvy & Mather began the 1990s under new ownership after Martin Sorrell's WPP acquired their shares in two transactions that came close to being called "hostile take-overs" by industry insiders. Subsequently, both agencies would be required to improve their profit margins at the behest of WPP.

Saatchi & Saatchi plc went through a management upheaval, with Maurice and Charles Saatchi leaving the company in 1995. Public ownership, delightful as it had been when everything was heading up, had its perils when profits and share prices went the other way. Saatchi & Saatchi's free-spending acquisition binge caught up to it, and the company's bottom line was hurt by over $1 billion in client defections associated with its program of agency acquisitions, which created client conflicts (Goldman, 1997, pp. 189-193). Shareholder dissatisfaction led to Board of Director actions, and the Saatchi & Saatchi management drama was played out in full by the British press.

Recession, advertising slow-downs, media spin-offs, procurement department investigations, client globalization initiatives, fee-based remuneration schemes and holding company ownership added significant complexity to ad agency operations by 1990. The simplicity of the Golden Age and the Creative Revolution was long gone, whether recognized or not.

There was more difficulty to come after 1990. It sneaked up on agencies in the form of a newly adopted corporate concept, "*shareholder value,*" defined as "*the value delivered to shareholders because of management's ability to grow earnings, dividends and share price – the sum of all strategic decisions that affect the firm's ability to efficiently increase the amount of free cash flow over time*" (www. investopedia.com).

Shareholder value became the mantra that boiled down corporate purpose to matters involving money, wealth and a performance obligation to owners – period. Boards of directors and executive compensation consultants used the concept to justify explosive increases in senior executive remuneration tied to improvements in corporate profitability and share price. CEOs used the concept to hire investment banks and strategy consultants to recommend and integrate mergers and acquisitions that added growth and incremental profits to their current companies. Procurement departments and their hired-in management consultants used the concept to initiate company-wide cost-reduction programs and to out-source entire departments to reduce corporate costs. Corporate raiders used the concept to criticize existing corporate leaders and to justify the acquisition and break-up of underperforming companies.

It was never mentioned at the time, but the widespread pursuit of shareholder value initiatives put marketing in the back seat among other strategic priorities. There were easier ways of growing the top- and bottom-lines than by gambling on marketing. Marketing was uncertain and difficult in the recession-prone, post-Golden-Age decades. The cozy relationship between chief executives and advertising agencies had unravelled, as other strategic advisers like investment bankers and strategic management consultants jumped to the head of the queue.

The shareholder value concept was originally attributed to economist Milton Friedman, who wrote, "The Social Responsibility of Business is to Increase its Profits" in the *New York Times Magazine* (Friedman, 1970). The concept finally developed traction in the 1990s, when executive pay went through the roof, as various compensation consultants and corporate advisors recommended higher performance-related pay to tie CEO actions to company marketplace performance. Companies quickly responded by handing out options and restricted shares to CEOs and other senior corporate executives.

In 1989, Michael Eisner of Disney performed as hoped for, and he earned $57 million based on a bonus formula that was applied to the pro forma financial results of the company. He delivered the promised financial results, and he had a generous bonus package in his contract that rewarded him for doing just that.

By 1990, there were seven "$10 million men" in corporate America (Crystal, 1991). A few years later, in 1994, Michael Eisner made $203 million. Sandy Weill got a pay package worth some $151 million for running Citigroup in 2000. Jack Welch's pay for managing GE in 2000 totaled about $125 million. Larry Ellison's 2000 pay as Oracle's chief was $92 million (Colvin, 2001).

The number one earners in each of the years 1995 to 2000 received packages valued cumulatively at nearly $1.4 billion, or $274 million on average (Colvin, 2001). By 2011, the average numbers were stratospheric – median pay of the US's 200 top-paid CEOs was $14.5 million (Popper, 2012).

Stock options were then the vehicle that fueled senior executive growth. Writing in *Fortune* magazine in 2001, Geoffrey Colvin reflected on the "highway robbery" of CEO pay: *"Although stock options had been available since 1950, the options culture began in the bull market of the 1980s. This made perfect sense since stocks essentially went nowhere from 1964 to 1982, and options during that past era didn't exactly make a CEO's heart beat faster. But once stocks took off, options suddenly became an excellent vehicle for getting rich, and companies began delivering them in truckloads. Besides, corporate raiders like Boone Pickens were arguing, rightly, that most CEOs didn't have enough skin in the game - they didn't own enough company stock to care about increasing the share price. Institutional investors and shareholder activists were pressing the same case"* (Colvin, 2001).

There were quicker ways to increase shareholder value than by investing in marketing and hoping that the investment paid off, particularly as consumer markets were becoming saturated and domestic growth was slowing down. Additional corporate profit growth could be achieved through financial engineering, cost reduction and mergers and acquisition (M&A) activities, and Wall Street advisers could provide the roadmap and the financing, particularly through junk bonds and other financial instruments. The payoff from financial initiatives was a big one, and it was significantly more certain than the payoff from marketing.

Writing in 2002, Robert Korajcyk of the Kellogg School of Management at Northwestern University identified 131 published papers from 1991-2000 on the subject of value-based management. The list included the highly influential 1991 book by G Bennett Stewart III, *The Quest for Value* (Stewart III, 1991), that preached the gospel of "economic value added (EVA)," defined as the profit earned by the firm less the cost of financing the firm's capital. According to the EVA theory, CEOs should maximize EVA on behalf of shareholders, and CEO compensation should be structured to encourage them to do so. In practice, CEOs who were paid on EVA principles had very elevated levels of compensation. EVA principles and publications provided the intellectual underpinnings used by board compensation committees to set and manage CEO compensation levels.

The obsession with quarterly earnings came about because personal compensation was increasingly tied to what happened to the share price. Improving market capitalization became the number one job for senior executives. Success would lead to personal wealth.

Sadly, as often happens with business ideas that make some people a lot of money, shareholder value caught on and became the conventional wisdom. Executives were only too happy to accept the generous stock compensation being offered. In due course, they even came to view it as an entitlement, independent of performance.

Moreover, an apparent exemplar of the shareholder value theory emerged: Jack Welch. During his tenure as CEO of General Electric from 1981 to 2001, Jack Welch came to be seen – rightly or wrongly – as the outstanding implementer of the theory, as a result of his capacity to grow shareholder value and hit his numbers almost exactly. When Jack Welch retired, GE had gone from having a market value of $14 billion to $484 billion, making it, according to the stock market, the most valuable and largest company in the world. In 1999 he was named "Manager of the Century" by Fortune magazine (Denning, 2013).

It was hard for ad agencies to influence CEOs, touting the latest "big creative idea" for television ads as the secret for corporate success. In addition, there was growing suspicion about the cost and effectiveness of television advertising, given the advances made in direct marketing and the exploitation of customer data through various CRM (customer relations management) database systems. There were direct and lower-cost, more effective ways of reaching the consumer, the direct markers said. Direct marketing and loyalty programs could provide more targeted messaging, but it required investing in a database of existing customers, tracking their purchase preferences and having retail data capture systems in distribution to monitor purchases. CRM systems lacked the glamour of big ideas, but they provided better measurability.

Direct marketing agencies, which previously were involved in direct mailing campaigns, began transforming themselves into customer data processing businesses, and they competed with their brethren traditional advertising agencies for marketing dollars. Increasingly, marketing total spend was less important than the *mix* of spend – some traditional, some direct – and later, some digital and social as well. The media alternatives grew and grew, and traditional advertising agencies no longer had the field to themselves. The choice between traditional advertising and direct marketing became known as the "above the line" versus "below the line" choice, based on an outdated accounting treatment of previously commissionable costs (above the line) and non-commissionable costs (below the line). Below-the-line advertising was growing faster than above-the-line advertising, and this was a cause for con-cern by the above-the-line traditional agencies, who were having their own problems breaking through "clutter" on the airwaves.

These debates took place far from client CEOs. Agency senior executives were still useful and needed in large relationships, coordinating the agency's creative work, but they were no longer striding the corridors just outside the CEO's office. There was nothing dramatic about the change in their status. There were no uncomfortable discussions. It was more like a marriage whose passion had faded. The compensation consultants, investment bankers and management consultants were hotter and younger, and they were driven to please in new and exciting ways. Their work generated increased share prices and increased profits – and helped to make senior client executives very rich.

The concept of shareholder value encouraged companies to cut costs wher-ever they could, and this responsibility was passed on to procurement depart-ments. They had had their hands full in the 1980s with manufacturing and distribution suppliers and costs, and as a result, media costs and agency remu-neration were then left alone. Later, though, during the 1990s and after 2000, procurement was increasingly directed to look at marketing and media costs.

Procurement did more than accelerate the shift from commission to fees. Once the fee system was in place, procurement could manage the fees for year-on-year declines.

The fee system divided agency remuneration into three "packages," and each of the three was subject to tough negotiations by procurement: 1) **Direct costs**. Direct costs were the salary costs of the agency people working on the account, plus statutory benefits, calculated by multiplying the headcount by the average salary and benefits rates. Procurement negotiated fewer heads and challenged average salaries, using "industry salary benchmarked data"[10] as their source of authority. 2) **Overheads**. An agency's total overhead costs divided by the agency's direct costs determined the "overhead rate." Typically, overhead rates were on the order of 100% or so, since overhead costs were approximately equal to direct costs. Procurement challenged the composition of the agency's pool of overhead costs, and disallowed certain items, like new business prospecting costs and holding company management fees. Procurement also used "industry overhead rate benchmarks," which were always lower than actual agency costs, to beat down agency overhead rates. 3) **Profit margin**. Finally, in the fee calculation, agencies submitted their profit margin expectations, usually in the range of 15% to 20%. Procurement often negotiated this downwards to 10%.

Thus, in the fee arrangement, agencies were paid on a cost-plus basis, with procurement seeing this as an opportunity to negotiate costs ever-downwards, as they had with other types of suppliers. [More accurately, agencies were actually paid on a "costs-as-procurement-defined-them" basis, which was certainly less than actual costs]. Unlike other suppliers with whom procurement had previously worked, ad agencies were generally uncooperative in providing data, and when they were pressed, they showed what was perceived to be an astonishing ignorance about the economics of their "ad factories," as some procurement people called them. Procurement assumed that the lack of cooperation was real but the ignorance was not; they assumed that agencies had something to hide, which was "extreme profitability" and "high degrees of inefficiency." Consequently, procurement felt safe in negotiating fees ever-downwards, even if the basis for this was arbitrary. As one automotive procurement executive told me "we whack their salaries or overheads by 10% or so if we feel that their numbers are soft. They protest, but they always accept it, so we must have figured them right – they've got plenty of fat."

The arbitrariness was widespread. Agency workload was not a factor used to justify agency headcounts. "Benchmarked data" were of questionable origin. Profit margins were arbitrarily selected. Year after year, post 1990, agency fees were chipped away, and the unbroken complaints from agency finance people about the "unfairness of it all" fell on deaf ears.

Looked at from an agency perspective, there was something unfair about the way agencies were being treated by their clients, and the unfairness was baffling. Weren't agencies still working hard to generate big ideas and create memorable ads? Weren't they safeguarding and building brand equity, helping to assure consumer loyalty well into the future? Weren't they expanding their capabilities from traditional advertising into direct marketing and providing "integrated services" for these two previously separate disciplines?

Yes, they were doing all these things, and yet their remuneration was eroding under the relentless questioning and assaults of procurement. It was easy to conclude that the deterioration in agency relationships was caused by these newcomers – these procurement people – who knew nothing about the subtleties of marketing, like consumers' emotional connections to brands, and who spread stories about agency inefficiency and phony accounting numbers among their peers at ANA meetings.

Was there nothing that could be done to neutralize these barbarians?

Procurement, though, was on a mission to support shareholder value. "Nothing personal," they could have said. "It's just business." Cutting fees was one of the new ways the game had to be played.

Agencies missed the significance of "shareholder value" and the change in priorities that it represented to their clients. They assumed, perhaps, that creativity and big ideas were eternal verities – that they were what clients needed under any circumstances. Shareholder value was just another management trend, buzzword of the month – nothing to worry about.

The management consultants did not see it this way. Early in the decade of the 1980s, as one example, Bain & Company adopted a mission statement that made "improved client results" as its single-minded mission. "Bain's mission," it said, "is to help our clients create such high levels of economic value that together we set new standards of excellence in our respective industries." That was a mission worth a CEO's attention and protection from procurement fee-cutting.

Shareholder value became, from the 1990s onwards, a driver of management consulting success and, somewhat sadly, of advertising agency marginalization.

CHAPTER 6 – THE RISE OF THE MANAGEMENT CONSULTANTS

"Somewhere out there, Patrick, is the key to increased sales. I want you to find that key, Patrick, and bring it to me."

Credit: Robert Weber / The New Yorker / The Cartoon Bank.

When "shareholder value" began to seriously influence CEO thinking from 1990 onward, there was an army of skilled management consultants ready to jump on board. We're interested in this subject here because the consultants had an indirect impact on advertising agency operations. Management consultants did not directly compete with advertising agencies, of course, but they did muscle in and dominate CEO time and attention while trying to improve shareholder value by working with CEOs and procurement departments on inefficient corporate processes and high costs.

With the passage of time, the management consulting firms grew and flourished, and as they expanded their mandates within their clients' organizations, they developed ideas about marketing strategies, channels of distribution, product pricing, media mix (traditional, social and digital) and other areas that might have been deemed to belong, in happier times, to the advertising agencies. This is evident today through any perusal of the consultant's websites[11], which are filled with insights and ideas about how marketing can be conducted in a more efficient and results-oriented manner.

Few advertising agencies today would see the consulting firms as direct competitors, and this is so – management consulting firms have yet to try their hand at creating or producing ads. Still, the consultants have had an important (and negative) effect on advertising agency client relationships, economics and prospects, even if this effect has been brought about through indirect rather than direct means.

I was a strategy consultant with The Boston Consulting Group in the 1970s and a partner and director of Bain & Company in the '80s, so I participated in the growth and expansion of each of these firms during their relatively early years. Later, after founding Farmer & Company in 1990, I worked with advertising agencies as their strategy consultant, seeing first-hand the kinds of pressures they were under from their marketing clients and related procurement departments. My consulting practice with advertising agencies and their clients has allowed me to observe and measure, first-hand, the ever-changing dynamics of their relationships with one another. This experience has provided the basis for this book – and given me the desire to document what I have seen and learned.

My experience with The Boston Consulting Group and with Bain & Company was enriching, to say the least. I joined BCG in early 1973, just 10 years after Bruce Henderson founded it. The firm then had about 100 consultants. In early 1979, I joined Bain & Company, six years after Bill Bain left BCG and founded this competing and very successful firm. Bain, too, had about 100 consultants when I joined, all of them in the company's single Boston office (by 2015, Bain had 51 offices in 33 countries). I was only somewhat aware at the time that BCG and Bain were leading *revolutions* in the way their clients thought about growth, profitability and investments among their portfolios of businesses. Instead, I was satisfied, as were most of my colleagues, to be working happily alongside one another in a stimulating environment that surfaced difficult corporate problems to analyze and solve. Only later, through the prism of 20-20 hindsight, was it obvious that the two decades of the 1970s and 1980s were a very special time to have worked in strategy consulting.

Author, editor and journalist Walter Kiechel documented the special character of the strategy consulting firms in his outstanding work, *The Lords of Strategy* (Kiechel, 2010). Kiechel focused on the ideas behind the growth and development of three firms (BCG, Bain, and McKinsey), and in the works of the famous business school thought-leader, Professor Michael E. Porter of Harvard Business School, author of *Competitive Strategy* (Porter, 1980), *Competitive Advantage* (Porter, 1985), and *The Competitive Advantage of Nations* (Porter, 1990).

Kiechel recounts the birth and evolution of *strategy as a paradigm* – a set of 1970s and 1980s ideas that refocused chief executives on the need to seek competitive advantage in the industries within which they competed. The focus on competition was new. In the search for competitive advantage, companies and their strategy consultants analyzed *costs* (relative to competitors), *customers* (pricing, segmentation and relative satisfaction), and *competitors* (relative market shares, corporate portfolios and ambitions) to determine a starting point; they then formulated and implemented action plans to achieve improved growth, profitability and competitiveness. BCG first developed and articulated the "price and cost experience curve" and the "growth-share matrix" in the 1970s[12] as diagnostic and conceptual tools; Bain developed and popularized "best demonstrated practices" in the 1980s to serve as performance benchmarks (Kiechel, 2010, p. 90); McKinsey developed in 1980 the "elements of a business cost system" as a guide to understanding all the cost elements that made up a product (Kiechel, 2010, p. 193); and Porter developed the "5 forces" (1980) and the "value chain" (1985) to add to the list of intellectual frameworks that underpinned the strategic paradigm (Kiechel, 2010, pp. 127, 196).

The conduct of strategic assessment and the development of strategic action plans was a highly analytical exercise. It required more than a bag of strategic tools and concepts – it required highly trained, data-hungry young consultants with first-class MBAs and (after 1990) personal computers with Excel and other analytical tools. The young consultants could operate successfully within their clients if they had sufficient "air cover" from the CEO, whose job it was to make sure everyone (*yes, everyone*) in the client organization cooperated with them. Gaining this kind of CEO support was a critical part of success in strategy consulting, and no one understood this better than Bill Bain, who articulated a confidential set of binding "client principles" to the Bain partners. Only those potential clients who met Bill Bain's highly selective criteria would be taken on.[13]

Strategy reshaped the concept of consulting and the kinds of people who practiced it, moving consulting from the realm of sage advice-giving by grey-haired industry experts to a world where business insights were *discovered in the data* by bright-faced hyperactive MBAs, whose only industry experience may have been in the consulting industry. Full credit for this reshaping must go to Bruce Henderson of BCG, who broke the mold and set the example through his early recruiting and marketing activities at business schools. Henderson valued high IQs and people who were intensely interested in data, concepts and ideas. In a famous recruiting ad for BCG in the Harvard Business School newspaper *Harbus* around 1969-1970, Henderson taunted the Harvard MBA student body: *"Are You Good Enough?"* The ad went on to describe the current consultants at BCG – their age profile (young), the percentage of consultants with PhD degrees (high), the percentage who had already published papers or books (also high), the percentage of valedictorians and honors graduates (nearly 100%), and so forth. The message was clear: BCG would hire only the best, the cream of the crop, and age didn't matter. Strategy consultants could be 23 years old if they were brilliant enough. Most of the HBS students scoffed at this display of BCG's arrogance, and the firm was then much hated (or much envied) on campus, but Henderson did not care about *most* of the students. He only wanted those who were attracted by the message, and in this he succeeded.

While the strategy paradigm was developing a head of steam in the '70s and '80s, advertising agencies were suffering a slight hangover after the growth and success of the Creative Revolution. The 1971 recession, followed by the energy shocks and recessions, caused most large agencies to suffer losses in total domestic billings (Fox, 1984, p. 314). However, media inflation was on the rise, and media commissions held steady in perhaps three-fourths of all agency-client dealings (Fox, 1984, p. 317). Importantly, this meant that agencies could operate as they had always operated, focusing on creativity and service, and agency account managers could continue to service their clients and sell-in the idea that their clients ought to spend even more on TV media – the kind of spend that generated agency income through media commissions. Nothing in the loss of domestic billings suggested that the fundamental business approach needed to be changed.

If there was any change going on at any of the agencies, it was in response to being acquired by a holding company and, separately, dealing with the shift from commissions to fees. In both cases, the attention of top management turned to internal operations and the shedding of excess costs – to meet aggressive holding company targets for operating margins on the one hand, and to respond to the beginnings of the fee declines triggered by the shift from commissions on the other hand.

There was a new trend for agencies to hire and parade before their clients "strategic planners," an ideal originally imported from the UK; but these were not strategists in the same way that management consultants were strategists. Instead, agency strategic planners were experts in customer segmentation and behavior, excellent at designing market research and reading the results of market research reports. The planners were called, in some quarters, "the conscience of the consumer" – they upheld long-term brand values on behalf of consumers and helped to resist any attempts by the creative department to go "off brand" in the pursuit of cute ideas that would dilute "brand values." In short, the strategic planners were consumer experts, brand developers and brand policemen. They were an important innovation, but they hardly signaled new strategic directions for ad agencies, and their efforts did not have the slightest impact on their clients' concerns about achieving improved shareholder value.

Ironically, the increase in numbers of the strategic planners had the effect of releasing the client service people from any previous responsibilities they had for brand strategic thinking – leaving them free simply to coordinate with their clients and give them all the service they needed.

One agency executive told me "the arrival of strategic planners signaled the final dumbing down of the client service department."

We should recall that during the commission era, client service people were relationship managers, brand guardians, strategists and salesmen – selling in the idea that clients should spend, spend, spend on TV media to steal a march on their competitors. In support of this, they were armed with research studies and Nielsen data that showed that big TV spenders tended to gain market share and succeed in their marketplaces. This was pure strategy – success was proportional to the degree to which clients outspent their competitors in a product category. What better justification could there be?

When commissions gave way to fees, though, client service executives lost their salesman role. Sure, they could continue to tout high TV media expenditures, but this time it made no difference to agency income or profits. Agencies were now paid on the basis of headcounts, and it was not so easy to sell the client on the idea that what they really needed were more agency people working on the account. Since workloads were neither documented nor tracked, the basic data to support this conclusion were missing in any case.

So client service executives became client servicers, and the arrival of strategic planners to shore up brand planning took substantive intellectual responsibilities away from them, further reducing their status in the eyes of their clients.

The contrast between the bright-eyed management consultants, who were working for the CEO, spreadsheets in hand, and the ad agency client service people, who were working for the marketers, could not have been more dramatic. Agencies were dismissive of the consultants, in any case. They looked askance at the MBA credential, finding that young men and women with MBAs, smart and analytical as they were, were also very expensive, and that kind of expense could not be easily borne in an environment where clients were cutting fees while holding companies were squeezing for more profits. Besides, there was nothing obvious in the skill set of client service people that required an MBA. The MBA made no sense at all to ad agencies.

It's fair to say that the management consultants tightened their grip on their clients as the strategy paradigm and the related shareholder value concept became corporate foundations. At the same time, advertising agencies began to slide down the slippery slope of their clients' organizations. Increasingly, procurement developed a louder voice in matters involving agency fees, CEOs disappeared as direct clients, marketing experimented with greater quantities of marketing deliverables across all media types and agencies responded, unsuccessfully, by over-investing in client service in an attempt to regain control of their relationships.

Whatever opportunities there were for agencies to become key players in corporate strategy and shareholder value by focusing on "improved results" was lost during this critical period. Agencies retained their primary cultural and commercial focus on "creativity and service," even though their market was shifting out from underneath them.

This lost opportunity has afflicted advertising agencies for more than 20 years. Even the advent of the more measurable digital and social advertising innovations was not enough to bring agencies squarely into the camp of those whose mission is solely to "deliver results."

CHAPTER 7 –
MEDIA EXPANSION, MEDIA FRAGMENTATION AND THE BALKANIZATION OF THE INDUSTRY

"This 'digital revolution'—can we muscle in on that?"

Credit: Robert Mankoff / The New Yorker / The Cartoon Bank.

Much is made today of big data in advertising, a new 'big' to worry about – The Big Bang, Big Foot, The Big Idea and now, Big Data.

Big data comprises the computer-analysis of consumer purchasing data and online behaviors to guide advertisers in their ad-creation and ad-buying decisions. One branch of big data leads to the development of new tools to permit more focused and programmatic (automated) ad buying, in which online and offline ads are bought through automated exchanges, often in real time. This is an entirely new development in recent (2013-2015) years. There are other uses and purposes of big data, most of them designed to improve the odds that John Wanamaker worried about – *"half the money I spend on advertising is wasted; the trouble is I don't know which half."* Big data is supposed to help decision-makers identify and spend on advertising that really works, and to increase the percentage of effective spending to levels well above Wanamaker's 50%.

Big data in its current incarnation is 'new' as of this writing, but it has existed less dramatically without a name for the past 50 years, for at least as long as accessible data processing and customer databases have been around. Computer power has always made it possible for clever people to find and crunch consumer data and draw conclusions accordingly[14]. What's new about big data is the quantity of consumer data available from online purchases, customer reviews, Twitter, Facebook, LinkedIn, Google Plus, Pinterest, Instagram, Yelp and other such sources. The internet, computing power and vast quantities of mineable information have come together in a "perfect storm" that has, for the moment, dominated discussions about marketing needs and marketing capabilities. Everyone is getting in on the act – IBM, in a recent ad in the advertising trade press, asked "How do leading organizations use big data and analytics to increase revenue, operational efficiency and more?" All you had to do was sign up for an IBM webinar to find out. There are many interested companies in the big data game, and they all are frighteningly competent when it comes to data crunching and analysis.

In many ways, new players have been the challenge in advertising for a long time. New capabilities and innovations appear to be specialized and distant from one another in the beginning, giving those with existing strengths a false sense of security, but over time advertising capabilities converge. Traditional advertising now competes with the formerly specialized direct marketing agencies, CRM agencies, and digital/social agencies. Computer programmers become highly desired agency resources. Is big data an area where data and analytical nerds will invade and dominate? Nerds can learn about advertising, and analyze customer data in order to make advertising more effective, but traditional advertising practitioners are unlikely to repay the complement and master what the nerds do best. The relative skills and capabilities are unequal. It's as if a one-way mirror was installed between the two groups – only one side can see through to the other, while the other is left staring at its own image.

The advertising landscape was once a homogeneous one, dominated by the traditional advertising agencies and the traditional advertising media in which they worked: print, radio and television. The traditional Mad Men and their creatives were the aristocrats of the industry, operating with big media commissions to carry out very visible and important work. Toiling at a lower level in the industry were the unwashed: the "below-the-line" practitioners of direct marketing and sales promotion, working in low-prestige below-the-line agencies, pencils behind their ears, estimating and bidding on local direct mail or promotional point-of-display projects that always went to the lowest bidder.

Apart from competing with one another for client dollars – *how much budget for above the line? Below the line?* – the two worlds co-existed and largely ignored one another. The traditional agencies certainly ignored the direct agencies, which were beneath them. The direct agencies ignored the snubs.

The below-the-line agencies had a number of things going for them, though. First, compared to the above-the-line agencies, they were able to measure the results from their work. If a mail shot of 100,000 letters went out at a known cost, and there was a positive response rate of (say) 2,000 letters (2%), then the benefits and costs were known, and the marketing ROI could be calculated.

Second, the below-the-line agencies were paid on a per-project basis, so they had to develop sound estimating, bidding and project-management skills. They were paid for all the work they did. Because margins were paper-thin in this highly competitive business, volume was key, and sales practices were sharp and aggressive. This package of skills never developed at the above-the-line agencies, even after commissions gave way to fees. Indeed, in 2015, above-the-line agencies are just awakening to the need for better project management capabilities, and they would consider being paid for all the work they do a small miracle.

Third, the below-the-line agencies were inevitably wedded to consumer and customer data, and technological and social developments were going to assure that data became more plentiful and powerful. History would prove to be on their side. Practitioners of heavy-duty data analysis, like Bain & Company's Fred Reichheld, were discovering and proclaiming the economic benefits of such things as increased customer loyalty, for example (Reichheld, 1996), and these efforts put an increased economic value on the development and exploitation of sophisticated customer databases.

Below-the-line agencies began to grow faster during the 1990s as advertisers lined up to experiment with improved CRM and loyalty programs. This phenomenon might have been overlooked by the traditional advertising agencies, but it did not go unnoticed by Sir Martin Sorrell and WPP, who aggressively acquired specialized below-the-line agencies, reasoning in a practical way that advertising might take several different paths in the future, so it was wise to have all the alternatives under one roof. By 2003, WPP owned well-known below-the-line agencies Wunderman and OgilvyOne, but it also owned A Elcoff & Co, Brierley & Partners, Dialogue Marketing, Einson Freeman, EWA, Good Technology, The Grass Roots Group, Headcount Field Marketing Group, High Co, Imaginet, FullSix, KnowledgeBase Marketing, Mando Brand Assurance, Maxx Marketing, rmg:connect, RTC, Savatar, sygyzy, ThompsonConnect Worldwide, VML and 141 Worldwide.

WPP identified a central feature of these specialized companies – they each loved working independently in their specialized fields, even though their clients had broader needs. Read here from the 2003 WPP Annual Report:

•   Our clients all live in competitive worlds. Whether Fortune 500 multi-nationals or single-nation charities, their first requirement, always, is an intrinsically appealing product.

- But for many years now, to compete successfully, they have needed more. They need access to high quality information, strategic advice and specialist communications skills. And it is in the nature of specialist talent that it is unlikely to flourish within the confines of a single marketing company. People of specialist skills work best and contribute more when recruited, trained and inspired by specialist companies.

- Within the WPP Group, our clients have access to companies of all the necessary marketing and communications skills; companies with strong and distinctive cultures of their own; famous names, many of them.

- WPP, the parent company, encourages and enables operating companies of different disciplines to work together for the benefit of clients and our people.

- There can be no doubt that discrete and sharply honed specialist talents working together with single-minded unity towards a common end is becoming a rapidly growing contributor to client success and therefore to group revenues (WPP, 2003).

In effect, WPP (like the other holding companies and the rest of the industry) accepted the Balkanization of the ad agency world as an accepted industry fact of life. Actually, "accepted" is less than accurate; the holding companies had a strong interest in maintaining the fragmented structure of the industry, if only for management convenience. Let's remember that the holding companies do not really manage their portfolio companies. They own them and establish annual profit targets for them. Once an agency or company is bought, and an earn-out arrangement has been struck with the current executives, the subsequent ongoing dialogue between the parties is about profit margin – are the current targets going to be met? Over time, the targets are raised, so there is always plenty to talk about, especially in view of declining industry prices – profit targets are always a stretch, and they always risk not being achieved.

As long as agencies or companies maintain their current structure, there is an unblemished historical record of operations and profits, from profit achievement in year one to profit achievement in Year 2014. If the portfolio companies in a holding company were merged or restructured, the historical record would be broken, and there would be new cost items ("reorganization costs") that would upset the growth of operating margins. Keeping companies as they were when they were bought makes life easier for the holding companies. This rule does not hold true for all portfolio companies, of course, especially where there are economies of scale, as in media buying, where there has been considerable merging of media companies. However, for the rest of the portfolio, fragmentation is how it was in the beginning, and fragmentation is how it remains today.

With a fragmented portfolio on the one hand, but a strong client need for integration on the other hand, the holding company must become the "integrator." The WPP argument in 2003 anticipated the "holding company relationship," much in vogue at this writing, whereby holding companies cut exclusive deals with major advertisers and provide all of the specialized agencies required for the highly varied SOWs.

Balkanization is a feature of the ad agency industry, but it is not a universal phenomenon across all service industries. Somehow, management consulting firms (again!) expanded their technical capabilities and specialties under one brand name. They added specialist consultants, to be sure, but at the same time, they expect their senior partners to become adept at understanding a growing number of disciplines. Senior consulting partners who manage large relationships with clients need to be multi-faceted – capable of working in mergers and acquisitions, cost reduction, organizational design, management information systems, corporate strategy and the like – and able to shift in and shift out of their assignments any required specialized resources. Indeed, one of the selection requirements for partnership in a consulting firm is an individual's intellectual capacity to learn and master a number of disciplines.

The cultural divides within the advertising industry became wider when web pages became part of the marketing mix, beginning in 1995. Early web pages were like printed catalogs, and traditional advertising agencies knew how to design catalogs – they were just pictures and words in a different medium, right? The rub was that web pages seemed to clients and agencies more like the domain of software folk, like computer programmers, rather than the domain of traditional copywriters and art directors. An automotive company that wanted to put up web pages to help consumers choose car models and features was more likely to go to a group of programmers than to a traditional agency. The web production costs were exceptionally high, too – the hours spent by web designers and programmers far outstripped the creative hours spent on catalogs. Wasn't the business of web design (and later, web advertising) a separate business?

Traditional (TV, radio, print) advertising agencies were quick to judge that the digital revolution was another specialty that would be handled by specialist agencies, just as direct marketing had been in the past. There was no comfortable place for programmers in the production department of an ad agency. Traditional advertising creatives could do the concept work for the look and feel of web pages, but the downstream execution, which was a digital production job, belonged elsewhere.

Technological innovation at the programming end, though, began to become the cart that drove the horse, and the question "what can we do with technology?" became as important a creative variable as images and sound. Digital technology did not really lend itself to a simple division of labor between creative (generating the ideas) and production (executing the ideas). In an increasing number of cases, creativity was all in the execution, especially in YouTube, Facebook and Twitter.

Balkanization in the advertising industry has limited the technical development of individual agencies and hobbled the intellectual growth of senior client service people. The downside of this is that each specialty has become less important for clients within their growing need for a mix of specialties, and that senior agency people have not grown intellectually to keep up with the changing needs of their clients. Advertisers today, requiring traditional advertising, direct marketing, PR, customer relationship management (CRM), events/sponsorship, social, digital, etc., have had to engage a broader number of advertising agencies. Each specialized agency in a manner of speaking has "lost share" within each client relationship, and each senior agency client head has lost influence with his/her client, as well.

Who, then, has stepped into the gap to manage these integrated needs?

- In many cases, clients have become their own integrators. This is the most logical outcome, since clients are dealing with increasing complexity as a matter of course, and this is simply one more of the many complexities. Self-integration is probably the right course for clients, but the practice is bad for the agencies; they are on the receiving end of directives rather than taking control and offering initiatives. Self-integration makes clients stronger and more self-sufficient, while it makes agencies weaker and dependent.

- In a few cases, clients have turned to lead agencies and asked them to be the "brand navigators," managing the loose network of diversified agencies on behalf of the client. This has been P&G's solution for the past decade or so, appointing brand account leaders (BALs) like Saatchi & Saatchi, Leo Burnett, Publicis USA and Grey to manage all the other agencies on a BAL brand (Pampers, Charmin, Tide and so on). Other advertisers have tried to emulate this structure with varying degrees of success.

- In a number of well-known cases (Ford, J&J, Bank of America), clients have entered into holding company relationships, but this means that all of the agencies come from a single holding company. It is not necessarily true that the holding company or a lead agency actually runs the integration, although this is the expectation.

- Finally, in very few cases, clients have required their agencies to expand their capabilities to cover a broad range of services, from traditional to digital advertising. Toyota and Lexus are two examples of advertisers who have gone relatively far in this direction with Saatchi & Saatchi and Team One, for example. In 2004, Toyota turned to its traditional (and virtually captive) agency, Saatchi & Saatchi Los Angeles, and encouraged the agency to hire digital specialists and to increase the proportion of digital executions within the marketing mix. From 2005 onwards, Saatchi & Saatchi invested in this capability, funded by fee levels that allowed them to do so, and by 2012, the amount of digital work was more than 50% of the total agency's marketing work. Ironically, though, this development within a single office did not spill over to other offices within the Saatchi & Saatchi network. It was an isolated instance of the agency responding to the request of an individual client, and its successful response did not lead the way for other such responses in other offices – mainly because other clients were not making the same kinds of demands or providing appropriate levels of fees.

The Saatchi & Saatchi Los Angeles example proves that Balkanization need not be the only outcome – agencies can become integrated across disciplines. However, integration is certainly the exception rather than the rule.

Balkanization of the industry has been the default outcome, driven by the agency belief that each agency discipline belongs in a separate house. Strategically, we can see that this belief has been shortsighted, having contributed to a loss of influence by individual agencies and an overall strengthening of clients in the relationship. The decline in agency remuneration, it can be argued, is one of the many consequences of the Balkanization of the industry.

SECTION II.
CONSEQUENCES

"Acceptance of what has happened is the first step to overcoming the consequences of any misfortune."

WILLIAM JAMES

"Have you always felt like a victim?"

Credit: Drew Dernavich / The New Yorker / The Cartoon Bank.

The big agencies had quite a ride during the 50 years from the Creative Revolution to the lean times of today. They survived the energy crises and related recessions of the 1970s, '80s, and '90s, cushioned by media price inflation. They went public and were snapped up by the marketing services holding companies, who began to hold them accountable for improved margins. They absorbed the early changes in remuneration from media-based commissions to labor-based fees by cutting back on their staffing levels. They had significant staff surpluses from the high-paying commission days when the use of multiple creative teams on client briefs was routine, so the first few years of resource cuts were not terribly painful – there was plenty of "fat."

Client globalization, the fragmentation of media and the rise of procurement departments were more complicated to deal with, since they weakened the agency grip on their clients and created internal management complexities, but agencies soldiered on after the millennium, cutting headcounts and holding the line on salaries to match fee cuts. SOWs, though, continued to grow.

After 2004, a line was crossed, when fees, resources and workloads were out of balance – fees were inadequate, workloads were excessive and surplus resources were gone, so the work had to be handled by stretched, cheaper people. For the next decade, the gap between workload and resources only widened, bringing us up to date with the highly stressed situation of today.

The documentation, tracking, and negotiation of workloads never became an agency priority despite the growing gap between workload and resources. The business-as-usual practice of offering unlimited service – or at least not complaining about clients' service expectations – continued, not only because that was the way things had always been done but also because agencies were afraid to upset the apple cart – to become more demanding with clients would have seemed suicidal, and few agency executives were prepared to take the risk.

The agency profit-equation was a complicated one: agencies had to earn 15-20% profit margins for their holding company parents, but a significant percentage of advertiser contracts generated less than this, with many of them at the 10% profit margin level.

The gap between holding company needs and advertiser contracts was relatively wide. Agencies knew full well that client contracts constrained their profits. The holding companies knew this as well, but their targets of 15-20% were non-negotiable, and agencies were expected to generate these higher targeted returns, no matter how difficult or impossible they might seem. Profit management was a senior executive responsibility at the ad agencies – perhaps the most important responsibility of all, if job security was at all important.

The pressure was mounting, even for the holding companies, whose results were influenced by their agencies' profitability. On February 27 2014,

The Telegraph headlined "WPP Shares Tumble on Missed Margin Targets," noting that "despite higher revenues and profits, WPP says margins are under pressure." The decline in share price wiped more than a billion pounds off the value of WPP after it admitted it would not increase profitability as much as it previously said. Sir Martin Sorrell, CEO, was quoted as saying "clients are very much focused on costs and wanting more for less."

Increased agency growth was touted as the usual solution for closing the profit gap. As one holding company finance director wrote to me on this subject: *"There are always ways [for the agencies to generate the required margins] but most agencies need growth to deliver. It is getting much more difficult. In markets where there is no growth, this is a serious problem."*

Growth from new business was not a realistic solution, since there was very little net new growth for an agency when new clients were won. The predominant agency belief that new clients were "incremental" to what they already had ignored the fact that clients in their portfolio tended to disappear routinely. Newly-won clients replaced newly-lost clients, and the new clients usually paid at lower rates than existing clients. Furthermore, agencies invested millions of dollars in the new business pitching process. Pitching, which was the principal high-status activity of senior agency executives, was a high-cost activity that generated low or zero profits for the first few years. Profits from new clients were illusive, and new clients did little to close the gap between holding company profit expectations and actual agency profits.

Since growth was not an immediate answer, agencies dealt with profit problems through cost reduction programs, hiring freezes and fourth quarter downsizings. They laid off a percentage of their people when all else failed.

As with all service firms, agency assets "ride up and down the elevator every day," as the cliché goes. With a reliance on hiring freezes or downsizings to make up for profit gaps, there were fewer people riding up and down, and with the long-term growth of workloads, these people were doing more and more work. They were increasingly junior, too – senior expensive talent was much less affordable.

One example of this is shown by the New York agency home office of "The Daedalus Agency" (disguised name) that we reviewed at various times between 2005 and in 2013. This agency office illustrates the workload, fee, resource and profit issues of the industry.

Let's look "under the hood" of The Daedalus Agency New York to see how management dealt with its challenges.

CHAPTER 8 –
AGENCY MANAGEMENT
OF RESOURCES
AND PROFITS

"I'll be leaving now, Williams... I've finished downsizing for the day."

Credit: Mick Stevens / The New Yorker / The Cartoon Bank.

The Daedalus Agency is owned by one of the major holding companies. Daedalus NY is its headquarters office. The New York office data (modified slightly for confidentiality reasons) for 2005 and 2013 are shown on the next page in Table 8-1.

In 2005, Daedalus NY had 10 clients who paid fees of $94,341,000 (Line 1). Daedalus NY assigned 275 people to these clients (Line 3). Eight years later, in 2013, Daedalus NY still had 10 clients, but three of the original clients had been lost and were replaced by three new clients who were won in competitive pitches. Despite these new client wins, Daedalus NY's fee income was 15% lower in 2013 at $80,046,753 – a reduction of $14,294,039 in income. In response to the reduced fees, the office downsized several times over the eight years, and the 2013 Daedalus NY headcount was down to 250 people, 9% below the 2005 level of 275 people (Line 3).

TABLE 8-1: THE DAEDALUS AGENCY - NEW YORK OFFICE FINANCIALS

Line #	Daedalus New York Office	2005	2013	Change
1	**Income (MM)**	**$94.341**	**$80.047**	**-15%**
2	**Number of Clients**	**10**	**10**	**0%**
3	**Professional Services Headcount (FTEs)**	**275**	**250**	**-9%**
4	*of which: Client Service & Planning FTEs (CS&P)*	150	115	-23%
5	*of which: Creative FTEs*	85	80	-6%
6	*of which: Production FTEs*	40	55	38%
7	**Client Service & Planning FTEs per Creative FTE**	**1.76**	**1.44**	**-19%**
8	**Professional Services Salary / Benefits Costs (MM)**	**$40.000**	**$34.000**	**-15%**
9	*Professional Services Costs as Percent of Income*	42.4%	42.5%	0.1%
10	*Professional Services Costs per Professional FTE*	$145,455	$136,000	-6%
11	*Overhead Costs (100% overhead rate)*	$40.000	$34.000	-15%
12	**Total Costs (Line 8 + Line 11) – MM**	**$80.000**	**$68.000**	**-15%**
13	**Operating Profits (Line 1 - Line 12) – MM**	**$14.341**	**$12.047**	**-16%**
14	**Operating Margin (Line 13 ÷ Line 1)**	**15.2%**	**15.0%**	**-0.2%**

The agency downsized by 25 people, down by 9% (Line 3), and reduced its professional services costs by $6 million, a 15% decline (Line 8). Creative headcounts dropped by five full-time equivalents (FTEs) and client service &

planning dropped by 35 FTEs, but production headcounts grew by 15 FTEs for reasons that we will discuss below. Professional services cost as a % of income increased slightly from 42.4% to 42.5% (Line 9). Average salaries (including 18% for statutory benefits) declined by 6% (Line 10) as the agency mix of people became more junior through downsizings, salary restrictions and selective hiring. Overhead costs, too, were reduced, from $40 million to $34 million (Line 11), but the overall cost decline of $12 million, down 15% (Line 12), was not enough to improve profitability. Daedalus NY earned 15.2% in 2005 and 15.0% in 2013, just meeting the holding company target profit margin of 15%.

So much for New York's *financial* performance.

What about the New York's *operational* performance? What happened to office workloads from 2005 to 2013? How were SOW workloads handled with reduced fees and reduced agency resources?

TABLE 8-2: THE DAEDALUS AGENCY - NEW YORK OFFICE OPERATIONS

Line #	Daedalus New York Office	2005	2013	Change
1	SOW Briefs (creative & strategic deliverables)	479	1,506	215%
2	SOW Workload (in SMUs)	340	465	37%
3	Fee Income (MM)	$94.341	$80.047	-15%
4	Fees per SMU (Price)	$277,473	$172,144	-38%
5	Professional Services Headcount	275	250	-9%
6	of which: Creative FTEs	85	80	-6%
7	of which: Client Service & Planning FTEs (CS&P)	150	115	-23%
8	of which: Production FTEs	40	55	38%
9	Resources Allocated (FTEs per SMU)	0.81	0.54	-34%
10	Creative Output per FTE (in SMUs)	4.00	5.81	45%
11	Client Service & Planning FTEs per Creative FTE	1.76	1.44	-19%

Note: SOW workload is measured in ScopeMetric® Units (SMUs), a Farmer & Company unit of work based on creative man-hours at an appropriate level of efficiency and productivity. An SMU is about the same size as a typical TV origination spot. See Chapter 11 for a more detailed explanation.

From 2005 to 2013, the agency's SOW deliverables for clients grew from 479 to 1,506 briefs (Line 1). I normalized the mix of deliverables in each year by converting each of them into ScopeMetric® Units (SMUs). The SMUs grew from 340 SMUs to 465 SMUs from 2005 to 2013 – a workload growth of 37% (Line 2)[16]. This net growth was the outcome of growth from existing clients, growth from new clients and workload declines from lost clients.

At the same time that net workload grew, office income declined from $94.3 million to $80.0 million, down 15% (Line 3). Fees per SMU, a uniform measure of price for the deliverables in 2005 and 2013, declined from $277,473 per SMU in 2005 to $172,144 per SMU in 2013 (Line 4). This decline was the actual price decline for the agency's work – a price decline of 38% over the eight-year period. That's a 2% compounded annual rate of decline, but even small rates like this have a large effect over time.

The production headcounts grew by 38% with 15 additional FTEs (Line 8) to produce the greater workload, but there were fewer creatives. Creative output increased from 4 SMUs per creative in 2005 to 5.8 SMUs per creative in 2013, a 45% increase in output per creative person (Line 10). That's a pretty astonishing increase in output per head, but it's typical of what I find in agency offices today.

The previously high client service and planning ratio (1.76 of these people per creative FTE in 2005) was reduced to 1.44 per creative FTE in 2013 (Line 11). This reduction meant that there was less account *coverage* for clients, but not necessarily a lower provision of client *service*. Given the pattern of growing workloads and reduced income, the agency was providing a lot more service – doing more work (some for free, evidently), and requiring additional efforts by the creatives and a greater amount of workload coordination by the client service people.

This agency office fairly reflects the ongoing situation in the industry. In my consulting practice, Daedalus New York is an example of what I find as a matter of course: growing workloads and declining fees, and accompanying headcount and salary reductions to generate profit margins for holding companies. As a consequence, creative outputs per head have been rising at a rapid rate, and agency offices feel increasingly stretched.

Are the creative output levels per head too high? By Farmer & Company measures, the appropriate level of creative output should be in the range of 4.1 to 5.0 SMUs per creative. When we established the SMU as a workload metric in 2004, we set its value at 4.1 SMUs per year – appropriate creative staffing without excessive re-work, rebriefing or the inordinate use of multiple creative teams. Why 4.1 SMUs per creative per year? I searched the industry for wisdom on creative productivity, but the only source I could find was David Ogilvy's *Ogilvy on Advertising*, written in 1983. Bemoaning the long gestation time for the production of advertising, Ogilvy wrote that "the average copywriter only gets three commercials a year on air" (Ogilvy, 1983). I assumed that this was for a typical mix of TV, print and radio ads.

I reasoned that if creative productivity was three ads in 1983, it was probably higher in 2004 as a result of pressure on agency remuneration and increased creative productivity. I applied a modest 1.5% compounded annual increase in creative productivity from "three ads per year" in 1983 over a 21 year period – and ended up with a creative productivity value of "4.1 ads per year" for 2004. I set this as my overall SMU creative productivity measure. Restating David Ogilvy's formulation, I would say "an average creative completes 4.1 ads per year in 2004." Interestingly, and consistent with the industry, Daedalus NY actually achieved 4.0 SMUs per creative in 2005, as shown above in Table 8-2.

By 2013, according to Farmer & Company consulting data, agencies were operating at creative output levels of 5 SMUs per creative per year – driven by the continued unit price declines from 2004-2013.

Daedalus NY's 2013 creative output was 5.8 SMUs per creative, or 16% to 41% above our standards. I believe that these creative outputs were too high and were adversely affecting creative quality. Creative outputs were certainly moving in the wrong direction. *Campaign,* the UK-based trade magazine, reported in 2013 that the average client-agency relationship dropped in length from seven years and two months (1984) to just two years and six months (2013). These findings are confirmed by research conducted by The Bedford Consulting Group in the US. Higher creative outputs per year are a fact, and so are shorter client relationships. Are these two facts related? I believe that they are.

AN OFFICE SNAPSHOT IN 2013

Back at Daedalus, ten clients generated the New York office's $80 million of revenue in 2013, involving 465 SMUs of work (for 1,506 deliverables) and the efforts of 250 agency professionals.

Of these clients in the office, Daedalus NY had three major clients that accounted for $56.0 million (70%) of the office's income. I've named them Client Alpha, Client Bravo and Client Charlie. The other seven small clients are at the other end of the alphabet: Client Tango, Client Uniform, Client Victor, Client Whiskey, Client X-Ray, Client Yankee and Client Zulu. Their details are shown below in Table 8-3:

TABLE 8-3: THE DAEDALUS AGENCY NY
– PORTFOLIO OF CLIENTS 2013

Client Name	Client Fee 2013	Resource Cost 2013	Resource Cost as % of Fee	Workload in SMUs
Client Alpha	$24,023,773	$10,946,303	45.6%	129.2
Client Bravo	$24,000,000	$10,116,397	42.2%	82.9
Client Charlie	$8,007,924	$3,834,362	47.9%	89.0
Client Tango	$4,804,755	$2,217,751	46.2%	73.9
Client Uniform	$4,800,000	$1,946,539	40.6%	21.9
Client Victor	$4,003,962	$1,640,949	41.0%	13.2
Client Whiskey	$4,000,000	$1,073,109	26.8%	26.4
Client X-Ray	$3,203,170	$1,042,075	32.5%	13.7
Client Yankee	$2,402,377	$733,908	30.5%	8.8
Client Zulu	$800,792	$448,606	56.0%	6.0
Total	**$80,046,753**	**$34,000,000**	**42.5%**	**465.0**

Daedalus NY allocated resources to each of these clients roughly in portion to client income in an effort to generate consistent profit margins for each client. This is a standard agency practice – resource costs are allocated to income, *which is a known variable*, but not to workload, *which is neither known nor measured*. As shown in the figures in Table 8-3, above, and in the graph in Table 8-4, on the next page, professional resource costs averaged 42.5% of income. The fee income of $80.0 million is 2.35 times the cost of agency resources, $34 million.

TABLE 8-4: DAEDALUS NY CLIENTS:
RESOURCE COSTS ARE PROPORTIONAL TO CLIENT INCOME 2013

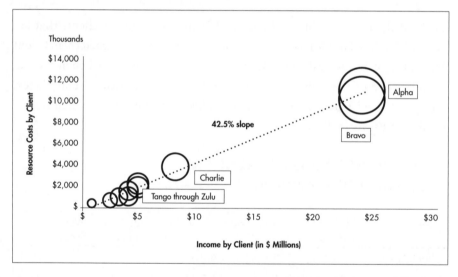

Note: circle size is proportional to client fees.

The practice that assigns resources proportionally to income assumes, it could be argued, that workload is proportional to income as well. If the three variables are proportional to one another, then the assignment of resources to income is as valid as the assignment of resources to workload, and the resources on one client are roughly as "loaded with work" as the resources on another client.

In an aligned agency world, client income, client resources and client workloads would be in harmony, balanced and proportional to one another:

Unfortunately, the agency world is not this aligned. Although income and resources are aligned with one another through a procurement-to-agency negotiation process, workload is a random variable – workload "happens" during the year through a separate marketing-to-agency process. As a result, there are very large disparities, client-by-client, with the workloads associated with client fees and resources. This is evident when we look at the relationship between fee income received and agency workloads by client. If we divide each of Daedalus NY's client's fees by workload (with workload in SMUs), the resulting number is "fee per SMU," or "price per SMU," and it varies considerably, by a factor of more than four times, from a high of $302,617 per SMU at Client Victor to a low of $65,010 per SMU at Client Tango, with an average of $172,144 per SMU across all clients. In a perfectly aligned world, by contrast, price per SMU would be uniform across all clients.

TABLE 8-5: DESIRED ALIGNMENT OF INCOME, RESOURCES AND WORKLOAD

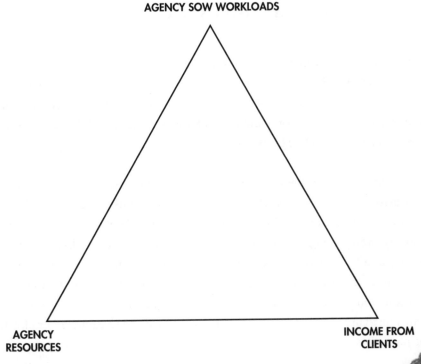

AGENCY SOW WORKLOADS

AGENCY RESOURCES

INCOME FROM CLIENTS

TABLE 8-6: DAEDALUS NY CLIENTS:
VARIATIONS IN PRICE (INCOME PER SMU)

Client Name	Client Fees 2013	Workload in SMUs	Price (Fees per SMU)	Share of Office Fees	Share of Office Workload	Average Price
Client Victor	$4,003,962	13.2	$302,617			
Client Bravo	$24,000,000	82.9	$289,589			
Client Yankee	$2,402,377	8.8	$272,226	78%	58%	$231,425
Client X-Ray	$3,203,170	13.7	$234,315			
Client Uniform	$4,800,000	21.9	$218,919			
Client Alpha	$24,023,773	129.2	$185,872			
Client Whiskey	$4,000,000	26.4	$151,672			
Client Zulu	$800,792	6.0	$134,574	22%	42%	$90,222
Client Charlie	$8,007,924	89.0	$89,985			
Client Tango	$4,804,755	73.9	$65,010			
Total	$80,046,753	465.0	$172,144			

The top six clients whose income exceeded the average price of $172,144 accounted for 78% of income, as shown in Table 8-6, but only 58% of workload (at an average price of $231,425), while the bottom four low-priced clients accounted for 22% of income but a substantial substantial 42% of workload at an average price of $90,222 per SMU.

Workload is random because it is not negotiated or planned with any rigor or consistency. A client's work is sometimes handled like a meal served in an agency's "all-you-can-eat" buffet, where fortunate clients can load up their plates without paying extra for second helpings, or it can be handled qualitatively as a list of work for which there are no measures – agencies have to guess about the resources they'll need. In other cases, it does not matter what is negotiated, because workload changes and grows, and remuneration remains unchanged because some clients turn a deaf ear to agencies' imploring for more fees.

Procurement sets fees based on a negotiated agreement about agency head-counts and costs, and (separately) marketing generates workloads for the agencies. Agencies, who measure client health through profitability measures alone, have no rigorous way to factor in client workloads.

TABLE 8-7: MISALIGNMENT OF INCOME, RESOURCES AND WORKLOAD

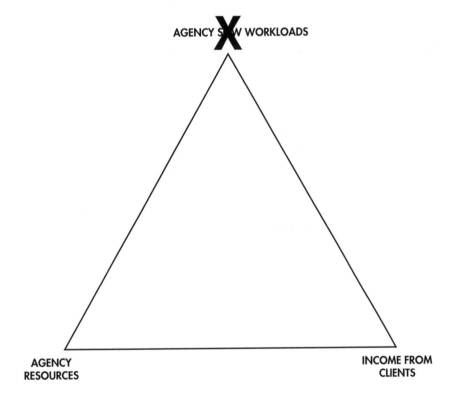

The misalignment of fees, resources and workload can be seen graphically by looking at a "portfolio of clients" in an agency office where client workloads are known.

In the graphic display (Table 8-8, over the page), the 10 Daedalus NY clients are shown as bubbles whose sizes are proportional to the fees paid by each client. The largest three clients, Client Alpha, Client Bravo and Client Charlie are shown as the three largest bubbles. The smaller seven clients are shown as smaller bubbles. The clients are distributed along the horizontal axis in accordance with price (fees divided by SMUs). Client Victor (a small client) and Client Bravo (a big client) have the highest prices (see accompanying data in Table 8-8), while at the other end of the spectrum, Client Tango (a small client) and Client Charlie (the third-largest client) have the lowest prices. Client Alpha, the largest of Daedalus' clients, has just an average price, and it's in the middle of the display.

The vertical positioning of the 10 clients is based on resource costs per SMU – the cost of the resources assigned to the clients divided by SMUs. In an ideal world, all clients would have roughly the same headcounts and resource costs assigned per SMU – on the assumption that "an SMU takes a given amount of people and cost" – but Table 8-8 shows us that this is not the case at Daedalus. Instead, high-priced clients get high resources, and low-priced clients get low resources *per SMU*. The difference in resources per SMU is more than 4:1.

The extreme differences in prices from client to client drive extreme differences in resource costs per SMU. The four clients on the left-hand side of the Portfolio of Clients have one-third to one-fourth the resource costs per SMU as the six clients on the right-hand side of the Portfolio.

TABLE 8-8: DAEDALUS NY: PORTFOLIO OF CLIENTS 2013

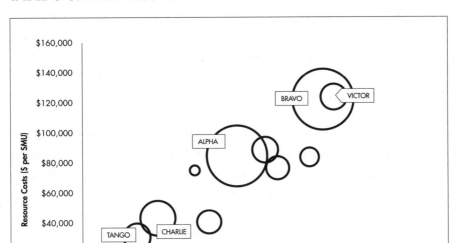

Client Name	Client Fee 2013	Resource Cost 2013	Workload in SMUs	Price (Fees per SMU)	Resource Cost per SMU
Client Alpha	$24,023,773	$10,946,303	129.2	$185,872	$84,692
Client Bravo	$24,000,000	$10,116,397	82.9	$289,589	$122,066
Client Charlie	$8,007,924	$3,834,362	89.0	$89,985	$43,087
Client Tango	$4,804,755	$2,217,751	73.9	$65,010	$30,007
Client Uniform	$4,800,000	$1,946,539	21.9	$218,919	$88,778
Client Victor	$4,003,962	$1,640,949	13.2	$302,617	$124,022
Client Whiskey	$4,000,000	$1,073,109	26.4	$151,672	$40,690
Client X-Ray	$3,203,170	$1,042,075	13.7	$234,315	$76,229
Client Yankee	$2,402,377	$733,908	8.8	$272,226	$83,163
Client Zulu	$800,792	$448,606	6.0	$134,574	$75,388
Total	$80,046,753	$34,000,000	465.0	$172,144	$73,118

More than once, I've heard a finance director say about a specific client, "Nothing to worry about – it's making a good margin." That might be the case, and if it's high-priced Client Victor, then the margin is to be applauded, but if it's low-priced Client Tango, then there's little cause for celebration. The statement "it's making a good margin" says very little about the client's actual situation. It could be great, or it could be terrible.

Tom Rosenwald, a prominent executive recruiter in the industry, told me, "Senior executives think and act the way they're paid." If achievement of profit margins is a major factor in ad agency pay, then senior executives will surely see their clients through a profit margin prism.

Agency offices look like the Daedalus NY office, with widely-distributed prices and costs that vary substantially from the left-hand poverty corner to the right-hand riches corner of Table 8-8. There are rich clients – the well-fed aristocrats of the office – and poor clients, the starving serfs, as shown below.

TABLE 8-9: THE OFFICE PORTFOLIO OF CLIENTS STARVING SERFS AND WELL-FED ARISTOCRATS

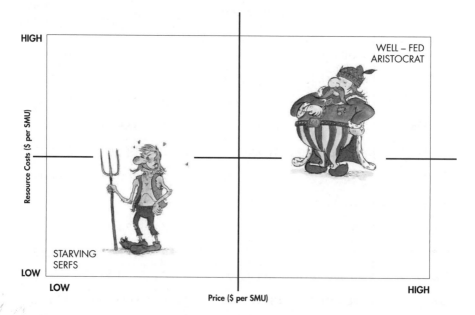

Over time, the Portfolio of Clients will deteriorate, shifting its center of gravity from the upper right-hand quadrant to the lower left-hand quadrant, as prices decline. You may recall from the introduction to this book that industry prices have been declining for more than 20 years, the outcome of growing workloads (growing between 2-3% per year, compounded) and declining fees (declining at 2-3% per year, compounded). Overall, this has led to a decline in industry prices of 4.5% to 5% per year, compounded. The average industry price of $400,000 per SMU in 1992 had declined to $150,000 per SMU by 2014. These figures are in constant dollars – inflation has been removed. See 8-10 below.

TABLE 8-10: PRICE CURVE 1992-2014 (PRICES IN $2014 PER SMU)

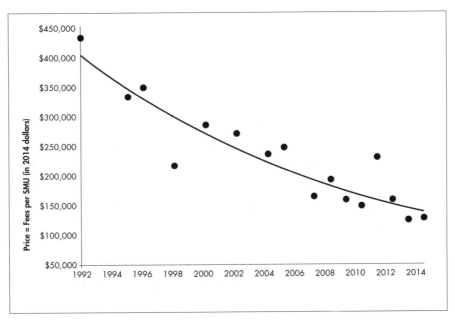

Source: Farmer & Company client data

This chronic industry price decline drives a deterioration in the quality of any portfolio of clients. Over time, clients slide downwards towards the left, as lower prices drive down costs per SMU, and well-fed aristocrats become starving serfs, as shown on the next page in 8-11.

TABLE 8-11: THE CHARACTER OF THE PORTFOLIO OF CLIENTS OVER TIME

The well-fed aristocrats in the upper right hand quadrant are gradually starved out of existence, and starving serfs become the agency norm, huddling in the poverty-ridden lower left-hand quadrant of the portfolio, underpaid and under-resourced. The downward drift brings about a decline and deterioration of agency capabilities, as the growing workloads are handled by fewer and more junior agency people.

Creative outputs per head rise as prices decline over time. The effect of pricing on creative outputs can be seen in Daedalus' 2013 client portfolio, shown on the next page in Table 8-12:

TABLE 8-12: DAEDALUS NY CLIENTS: CREATIVE OUTPUTS (PER HEAD) ARE DIRECTLY AFFECTED BY PRICES

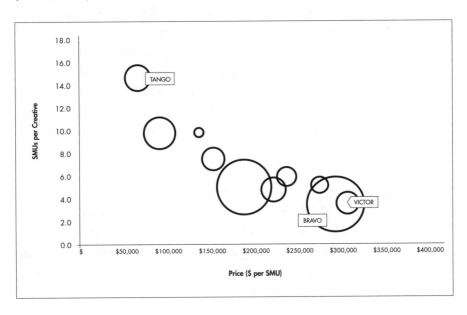

Client Name	Workload in SMUs	Price ($ per SMU)	Creative Headcount	SMUs per Creative
Client Tango	73.9	$65,010	5.0	14.8
Client Zulu	6.0	$134,574	0.6	9.9
Client Charlie	89.0	$89,985	9.0	9.9
Client Whiskey	26.4	$151,672	3.5	7.5
Client X-Ray	13.7	$234,315	2.3	5.9
Client Yankee	8.8	$272,226	1.7	5.2
Client Alpha	129.2	$185,872	25.8	5.0
Client Unifom	21.9	$218,919	4.6	4.8
Client Victor	13.2	$302,617	3.7	3.6
Client Bravo	82.9	$289,589	23.8	3.5
Total	465.0	$172,144	80.0	5.8

The range of creative outputs per creative head in 2013 was very broad, from a high of 14.8 SMUs per creative (Client Tango) to a low of 3.5 SMUs per creative (Client Bravo). This difference was not due to differences in the characteristics of the respective SOWs. Client Tango did not have a less complicated mix of work that explained its exceptionally high productivity. Client Tango cranked out more than four-times the creative output as Client Bravo – it had to, since its price ($65,010) was about a fifth of Client Bravo's ($289,589). Client Tango was a client with low price and high creative output per creative, whereas Client Bravo was a client with high price and low creative output per creative.

Under the pressure of a 37% workload increase from 2005 to 2013, and with an income decline of 15%, Daedalus NY had to increase its creative productivity from 4.0 to 5.8 SMUs per year. That's a 45% increase in productivity over eight years. Unless this trend is halted by agency management, then future increases in creative productivity will be required at an accelerated rate. This is sure to be accompanied by a decline in creative quality.

That Daedalus NY does not have a healthy portfolio of clients should now be evident to the reader. Its future portfolio is likely to be even less healthy unless Daedalus NY's top management team sets out to put a floor under declining prices and unpaid workload growth.

CHAPTER 9 –
THE (OUT-OF-DATE)
SELF-ORGANIZING
AGENCY

"Remember, 'accounting' and 'accountability': nothing in common."

Credit: Leo Cullum / The New Yorker / The Cartoon Bank.

Daedalus NY needs to mobilize to put a floor under falling prices, as discussed in the previous chapter. The alternative is to surrender to the inevitability of continued price declines and the destructive stretching of agency resources. Daedalus NY is one office of many in The Daedalus

Agency; its problems are a microcosm of the agency and, at least in my experience, of many offices and agencies in the industry. I've seen this over and over again, in the US, Canada, UK, France, Germany, Italy, Spain, Brazil, Turkey, Russia, Thailand, Philippines, India, China, Singapore and Australia, just to mention a few places.

Price is mathematical – it's income divided by workload. As long as workloads grow faster than income (or income grows slower than workloads), price will decline. Thus, there is both a "workload imperative" (*get workload under control*) and an "income imperative" (*get paid better for all the work that is done*).

These are not easy problems to solve. *Workload growing faster than income* is the default industry condition:

1. **Advertiser marketing experimentation with new media will continue**. As effective as mass advertising media have been – and nothing has ever matched TV for its ability to reach large audiences – digital media promises mass customization, permitting the possibility of reaching a large number of individual consumers with tailored messages at lower cost with less waste. The hope is that improved targeting will be more effective, leading to improved brand growth. With increased innovation and the evolution of digital technology, experimentation is the name of the game for advertisers. Consequently, marketers will continue to experiment with digital advertising and social engagement programs without making compensating and equivalent cuts in their traditional media spend. This tendency will drive continued workload growth.

2. **Aggressive procurement practices will continue, and fees will be cut accordingly**. Procurement departments live and breathe cost reduction. They're inclined to see marketing expenditures as *costs* rather than investments. Procurement worships the god of shareholder value. Procurement believes that agencies are fat and profitable, and they note, in support of this belief, the glowing reports of holding companies when profits are announced[17]. *Overall, procurement is motivated to drive down agency fees and income.* No effective argument has been posited by agencies

to neutralize procurement's behavior. Agencies have not, for example, shown that greater investments in marketing would give disproportionately greater returns to their clients. Few agencies have made persuasive arguments about the mismatch of fees and workloads. Consequently, procurement's attitudes are set, and they are reinforced at industry conferences. It will take a large effort to change their attitudes and behavior.

3. **The agency self-image as a** *"provider of creativity"* **will continue**. The *creativity paradigm* leads agencies to focus on "creativity" as their relevant output rather than on the growing tangible volume of work that they actually produce. If agencies could see themselves instead as *"creative developers and producers of marketing deliverables,"* they might have a greater sensitivity about workload volumes. Instead, they are allergic to the idea that they are "delivering measurable stuff." As a result, they don't measure how much stuff they commit to or how much stuff they do. Continuation of the allergy will surely favor the continued growth of agency workloads faster than income. It will take not only executive energy but a change of mindset to reverse this trend.

Agency turnaround plans must be developed by agency top management teams and carried out with vigor throughout their agencies, with a goal to develop the full support and engagement of client heads and their client service teams. This will not be easy, since these plans will require an executive leadership style that has little precedent in most agencies' history. The requirement for senior executives to *manage agency operations* with a tougher mindset is inconsistent with the laissez-faire style associated with *agency self-organization*, which has been the traditional way agencies have been run to date.

Leadership style is not the only challenge. There is a "followership" challenge as well, in that agency people are used to being unmanaged rather than being reviewed and held accountable. Agency executives may initiate a new style of leadership, but getting agency people to follow will be difficult. The most important required followers are client heads and their client service teams. Today, these folks have a lot of latitude to do whatever they want and define their jobs in whatever way they wish, subject only to client requirements.

They will resist management efforts. The resistance will be partly intellectual (*tight management will kill our creative culture*) and mostly self-serving, since they will not like the prospect of being managed. They're quite prepared to be managed by their clients, and to salute when a client needs something, but they can be expected to resist when their own executives try to tighten things up.

Let's not, then, view this as an easy turnaround. Agency executives will have their hands full. They will need to charge ahead without wavering, and reward those who follow and deal with those who resist in a firm way.

THE HEAVY LEGACY OF BILL BERNBACH

The agency allergy to measuring work has a long history, but we only have to go back to the early 1960s to find a grand figure who not only wrote about it but may have influenced several generations of agency executives.

The grand historical figure is none other than Bill Bernbach.

Bill Bernbach (1911-1982), the renowned founder of Doyle Dane Bernbach (DDB), has a special place in industry history for his creative innovations on behalf of Volkswagen, Avis and Alka-Seltzer – ads that were the backbone of the Creative Revolution, described in Chapter 2.

He is also remembered for his quotations, which surely helped to establish the *culture of creativity* that continues to dominate agencies today:

• *"Properly practiced creativity must result in greater sales more economically achieved. Properly practiced creativity can lift your claims out of the swamp of sameness and make them accepted, believed, persuasive, urgent."*

• *"Nobody counts the number of ads you run; they just remember the impression you make [18]."*

The 1950s and 1960s world of Bill Bernbach no longer exists, but the Creative Revolution still shapes agency thinking even though *creative* advertising is no longer the novelty it was 50- to- 60 years ago. TV advertising is just as likely to be skipped as ignored by today's ad-weary consumers. Agency prices are only 25% of what they were during The Golden Age; doing unlimited work is no longer economically feasible.

The fact that nobody counts the number of ads that an agency completes is regrettable. One can't really blame Bill Bernbach for this – what he meant was obvious and relevant for the Creative Revolution time period. However, the advertising industry has since moved on, and the fact that ads are not counted or measured is now a major strategic problem.

ADVERTISER VS. AD AGENCY MANAGEMENT CULTURES

The enemy is *"workload growing faster than income."* The advertisers' teams are well-organized and relentless. Among other things, marketing and procurement executives get together at ANA conferences and share *"best practices."* These *best practices* focus (in part) on cost-reduction subjects, including how to reduce agency fees, what kind of benchmarks to use, whether or not to establish internal ad agencies, whether or not to take production responsibilities away from agencies, and many others. The discussions certainly have the effect of stiffening the backbones of marketing and procurement executives, making them stronger and tougher when they think about negotiating with their ad agency partners. Furthermore, these executives work and operate in cost-conscious, performance-focused corporate cultures where accountability is a fact of life, and reviews of performance are routine. A certain amount of tough-mindedness flourishes in corporate settings.

This does not mean that advertisers are well-organized and disciplined in their day-to-day dealings with agencies. On the contrary: advertiser briefing and ad approval processes are often very poor, and SOW planning processes are almost non-existent. Months can pass before contracts are signed, and out-of-scope deliverables pop out of nowhere, like dandelions on an uncut lawn.

This kind of disorganization should not fool agencies into thinking that advertiser cultures are disorganized and undisciplined. To the contrary, there's a lot of corporate backbone throughout the marketing and procurement organizations. Client disorganization, such as it is, allows clients to get something for nothing. There's more method to madness in their disorganization.

Agencies' organizations and cultures could not be more different from their clients'.

Accountability for agency operations is fragmented. Each office in a network is a separate profit center. Each department in an office self-defines its missions. Creative heads focus on creativity; finance directors focus on headcounts, overhead and budgeted/actual costs and profits; client heads manage the service that they provide to their 'disorganized' clients and keep them coming back for more. (Despite this there seem to be very *few* happy clients.)

Managing service levels means a number of things: obtaining internal or freelance resources when workloads require additional capacity; rescheduling deliverables; handling rework; agreeing to new client SOW priorities, including new or repositioned work – but client heads do not really manage SOWs in a proactive way. They do not, as a rule, hold the line on scope creep. They respond. They mobilize their teams to deliver whatever they have to deliver. For many client heads, this is the essence of their job: appeasing their demanding, disorganized and grumpy clients. The miracle is that they achieve this in the face of resource constraints. The downside of the miracle is that their success is killing their own agencies.

Their "bosses" – the agency, regional and office CEOs – leave them alone, for the most part. They do not review their performance. They do not discuss SOWs. For the most part, their bosses are out in the marketplace, drumming up new business, seeking new clients as a way to shore up growth and deliver promised revenue and profits to the holding company.

Who is responsible for an agency's operational response to growing workloads and declining fees? In today's agency culture, it's everyone….and no one. The agency management culture is fragmented and divided. Everyone does his/her own thing. An integrated counter-attack is hard to organize, and in practice, it simply does not happen. At the end of the year, the finance director has the ultimate responsibility to deliver the agency's profit margin, and this is often done through cost reductions – a blunt instrument, indeed, but the laissez-faire culture does not allow for much fine-tuning during the year.

The agency management culture is a barrier to change.

It is virtually unchanged from the management culture of more than 50 years ago, reinforced by the Creative Revolution, when the agencies were rich and the creative departments accepted no masters. Agencies could operate as businesses without much active management as long as they could keep their commission-paying clients and add a few new ones every year.

Agencies retain a perverse but understandable pride in the unmanaged culture that is associated with "being creative."

As Kevin Roberts, CEO of Saatchi & Saatchi described it to me in 2014: "*We don't believe that anyone can run a first-rate creative shop with organizational diagrams and spreadsheets. That kind of Bain-and-McKinsey stuff would kill our creative capability. A creative agency needs to operate more like an ant colony, where every ant knows its job and has the freedom to do it.*[19] *As long as we hire and inspire the right people, to do the right thing, to build our clients' business and market shares, our agency should grow and our creativity should flourish. If we take another approach, like a typical command-and-control company, we'll end up in the dustbin of mediocrity. I still believe in hiring Mad Men rather than Math Men.*"

Although agencies have seen considerable changes in their operating environments – the rise of holding companies, the change from commissions to fees, the empowerment of procurement, the globalization of client relationships, the development of new digital and social media and the fragmentation of their client relationships – they have been constant in their commitment to self-organizing management cultures that celebrate creative departments and allow other individuals to define their own rules and priorities.

How does self-organizing actually work in the typical agency? We know what the creatives and production people do. What do the other "ants" do?

CLIENT HEADS AND CLIENT SERVICE TEAMS

Collectively, client heads and client service executives are the custodians of 100% of agency income. They approve 100% of the agency's strategic and creative workloads, and they use 100% of the billable capacity assigned to them.

Client heads have vague and unwritten job descriptions. This was not the case during the commission era, when a client head's clear mission was to get the client to spend large amounts of money on commission-paid media. The change from commission-based remuneration to fee-based remuneration change was momentous for client heads – they ceased to be media salesmen on behalf of the agency. Today, it is assumed that client heads understand their revised responsibilities, which can be described as *"please your clients, hang on to client income, and do the best you can to deal with client demands and disorganization."*

This definition captures what has been a long, slow decline in agency responsibilities for client heads. Client heads and their client service colleagues were previously the activist and aggressive "owners" of their commission-paying clients during The Golden Age, fighting off all client attempts to cut media spend or bring in other agencies. Since then, client heads have lost a lot of their aggression, and since the change from commission-based to fee-based remuneration, no one has quite redefined what their new muscular roles ought to be.

Furthermore, client service responsibilities have become divided, especially after 1980, first through the widespread adoption of a British innovation, "account planning". Agencies created "account planners," who were tasked to do a better job of bringing consumer insights into advertising – a role in which that client service people were deemed not to be sufficiently expert. Account planning (today called strategic planning) was brought to the US by Jay Chiat in the 1980s and spread throughout the industry. Strategic planners number approximately 20 FTEs for every 100 client service FTEs. The strategic planning innovation reduced the responsibilities of client service executives and put strategic planners at center stage with respect to advertising development.

More recently, client service responsibilities have been divided again through the creation of agency project managers, who are believed to do a better job "project-managing client work through the agency." Project managers were a recent (post-2000) response to the chaotic and costly way that client work was being shepherded through agencies' creative and production departments. This type of coordination used to be solely the responsibility of client service people, and it gave them bully rights over the creative and production departments – account managers were the guys and gals who pushed the work through these overworked departments.

No more, at least at this writing. Agencies hope that project managers and project management systems will bring some order to the flow of workload through the agency (the jury is out on this issue, as best I can tell – project managers have even less accountability than client service people).

Client heads and their client service teams, then, have been downsized and downgraded over the past decades – responding to changes in remuneration and to perceptions that their generalist skills were not quite good enough to deal with advertising research and project management.

In the 2014 era of big data, the perception that client service people are not quite up to the analytical task is a new theme. At the March 2014 4A's conference in Los Angeles, advertisers and agencies sparred over agency access to clients' brand data. Clients expressed concerns that agencies "could not be trusted" with this sensitive data. Others expressed concerns that agencies were insufficiently analytical. "It's not the data itself that's the advantage," said a Google executive. "It's the insights." That only works if agencies have the skills to derive insights from data. "My challenge to agencies is to say, 'Use my data to be proactive,'" said one CMO. "But I struggle and worry you don't have the talent." (Marketers, Agencies, Google Spar Over Brands' Precious Data, 2014)

What client heads and their client service teams are left with today is "servicing the client and responding to demands," doing their best to manage client expectations and needs for creative and analytical work.

It is assumed that "doing their best" will generate profits, but client heads and their teams are under no "do or die" imperative to ensure that profits are 15% or greater. Each client head can make excuses for why targeted profits cannot be earned:

- *The price was set by the holding company or the CEO. I can't do anything about it.*

- *The contract is for 10%, not 15%. I can't change the contract.*

- *The client will only pay for an agency team of 15 FTEs, and that's it – they won't pay for the 20 we need.*

- *My job is to get the work done within these limits.*

Clients are viewed as unmanageable constraints on agency performance, like spoiled children. Client heads are like nannies or babysitters who believe that the brats are beyond saving. It's easier to give in than to fight. It's also less risky. Who wants to lose a client over an argument? Who wants to lose a job?

Each client head has fully-delegated authority to manage his/her clients in any way that he/she sees fit. Each can approve out-of-scope work, whether or not it is paid for, and use agency resources, whether or not their costs are covered by client fees. They can plan SOWs or let their clients plan them for them. They can negotiate aggressively or simply give the client the service that the client wants. They can manage their resources tightly or loosely.

In the meantime, in background, strategic planners go about their job, helping to bridge the gap between clients and agency creatives on consumer research matters, while project managers help to schedule and push the workload through the various agency departments.

However client heads handle their client situations, they can be sure that what they do today will be relatively invisible to senior agency executives.

The way that client heads go about their management job is not measured or reviewed. There are no metrics other than profit margin to differentiate between who is doing a good job and who is not. There are no standards for the client head. There is no defined *"Agency Way"* for managing clients. The job is left up to the individual initiatives of the client heads, who carry out their responsibilities without a rule book, set of standards or measures.

Client heads are responsive to clients and generally unresponsive to agency initiatives that interfere with their freedoms. Client heads are not interested in transparency. They do not want their actions exposed and visible. They simply want the freedom to act and service. If they do a good job keeping the client on board, they create job security for themselves.

This is the agency culture, developed and reinforced for more than 50 years. Client heads each "run" part of the agency, and the total agency is simply the sum of their actions, whether the actions are known or not and whether or not the actions are strategically good for the agency.

Client heads do not wish to make trade-offs or to say "no" to their clients in order to promote agency interests. To do so would represent a major change in attitude and a shift in the center of gravity away from client interests towards agency interests.

No one is telling them that this is what must happen.

CHAPTER 10 – THE RESULTS-FOCUSED PARADIGM

"Good news—I hear the paradigm is shifting."

During the Creative Revolution in the '60s and '70s, highly creative agency work was designed to drive client product growth rates, and to do a better job than the hard-sell 'unique selling proposition' (USP) ads that had been current in the industry.

This strategy was successful and agencies were well-rewarded for their efforts – clients spent growing amounts on media, and agencies reaped growing income from their 15% media commissions and from winning new clients. All the evidence from this period, about 50 years ago, suggests that the Creative Revolution was successful in delivering results and rewarding agencies at the same time. New highly-creative agencies like Wells Rich Green (1966) entered the market and took clients away from their less creative competitors; industry growth rates were strong, driven by higher client media spends, and during this period, many agencies went public, based on strong and growing top and bottom lines. Creativity was unique and highly visible; agencies perceived as highly creative were "hot" and in demand.

However, the worlds of 1960 and of 2014 are very different. We've had 50 plus years of these *creative* ads; the originality of this type of creativity is long since gone. What might have been seen to be "edgy" and creative in the 1960s would be "ho-hum" today. In the current era, too, the media mix is much more diverse, and the amounts spent on creative experimentation – mostly through social and digital media – are very large and diffuse. The volume of creative output has grown exponentially. We're well beyond the time when pure creativity could be focused on television advertising and deliver dramatic changes in brand results. It's now harder to assess the impact of creative efforts; creativity is one of many factors that drives success. Advertisers are increasingly concerned about the need to identify *all* the factors that drive marketing ROI. The development of tools to measure ROI is a current preoccupation, and the large investment in digital marketing has both accelerated the preoccupation and provided hope that through the magic of "big data" ROI solutions can and will be found.

The corporate obsession with "shareholder value" is a major factor, and it gives further urgency to the quest to find marketing ROI solutions. Advertisers want to make sure that marketing expenditures contribute to the realization of increased shareholder value. John Wanamaker's observation that *"half the money I spend on advertising is wasted; the trouble is I don't know which half"* begs, with increasing urgency, for the need to find and eliminate the non-value adding half. Procurement ignores the theoretical 50/50 split between wasted and non-wasted expenditures and attacks, with vigor, all fee expenditures, particularly the expenditure on agency fees.

Procurement people are skeptical about current levels of marketing expenditures – they believe, as an article of faith, that all marketing expenditures are chronically inflated and excessive. Supporting their skepticism is a belief that agencies have done very little to provide results-based arguments to defend the effectiveness of agency contributions and the reasonableness of agency fees.

Traditional agencies (in particular) continue to highlight *creativity* as their most distinguishing characteristic. Since this speaks less to client concerns, their bragging about creativity is really an inwardly-focused narcissistic exercise that distracts agencies from more relevant client priorities. We've discussed this subject in previous chapters. Our argument is not over the need for creativity in agency work. Creativity is to ads as product quality is to cars, airplanes and electronic equipment – it's absolutely necessary, and it needs to be built-in to the product, but it is not the only factor that matters, and it hardly provides sustainable differentiation from one agency to another. True, one agency will be "hot" for a given period and will grow and win business (one thinks of Crispin Porter + Bogusky or mcgarrybowen in recent years), but then the wheel turns, and the hot creative agencies of today become targets for other upstarts – and are eventually superseded in the same way that professional tennis stars are eventually vanquished at Wimbledon. The great bulk of the actual creative work in the industry is done by non-hot agencies, in any case, and hot agencies are more notable for the amount of trade-press ink that is devoted to their hotness than for their actual impact in the marketplace. Hot agencies are paid no better than non-hot agencies, even if during their moment in the sun they may be more profitable because their fee growth exceeds their overhead cost growth.

Agencies need to refocus on their clients' needs and acknowledge that the creative paradigm does not deliver the same kind of dramatic brand results that it did 50 years ago. Its value has declined substantially if we measure it by the average price that clients are prepared to pay. If pure creativity continued to deliver the kind of results that it did in the past, then agencies would be paid much more than they currently are – improved client results would most certainly justify higher agency fees.

Agencies need to refocus their thinking and *to organize themselves to maximize the probability that their work will generate improved results for clients*, aligning themselves with their clients' preoccupation with *increased shareholder value*. We believe that this will require a very substantial change in the way agencies organize and think about themselves, particularly in the way that senior agency executives define their roles and the way that client heads and their colleagues in client service employ their skills and carry out their responsibilities, particularly with respect to SOW matters. It means that "creativity" can no longer serve as the rallying cry or key factor by which agencies identify themselves to clients, potential clients and their own people.

What does it mean for agencies to *organize themselves to maximize the probability that their work will generate improved results?* It's one small step short of organizing themselves to *guarantee* results, because guarantees are simply not possible. It's a giant step away from thinking only about being a good service provider and being creative. Instead, it's a giant step towards creating intimate strategic partnerships with each client, basing them on mutual commitments to seek improved results and increase shareholder value.

Agencies need to initiate the creation of *marketing and strategic performance partnerships* that see themselves and their clients as co-equal partners, each with specific responsibilities and roles, each of them committed to finding successful, results-generating marketing paths for the advertisers' brands.

Shared commitment. The commitment is best captured in a short document that could be called "principles of a relationship between [agency] and [advertiser]" (fill in the appropriate names) and signed by the two parties to indicate that it is a contract of mutual expectations. The document should be structured around a number of key governing assumptions:

1. **Focus on results**. The relationship is designed and structured to bring about improved market performance for advertisers relative to their cur-

rent and potential customers at the expense of their competitors. This means, in the most general terms, improved growth and profitability, gains in market shares and strengthened brand equities.

2. **Become a partner**. In these relationships, ad agencies are the advertiser's "marketing and strategic performance partners," expected to propose, deliver and execute marketing communications that have the highest probability of achieving agreed performance-improving goals.

3. **Make a mutual commitment**. Each party has an expectation that their relationship will become a committed, long-term relationship that will endure by virtue of the value and satisfaction that it generates for both parties.

4. **Structure for flexibility**. The relationship will be structured for flexibility and experimentation. The route to marketing success in today's environment involves thoughtful judgments about what *should* work, with ongoing experimentation and constant adjustment to exploit what can be learned. As a result, the relationship must be structured to permit fast, flexible and committed adjustments to agreed marketing plans.

Respective and joint responsibilities. In addition to accepting these key assumptions, agencies and their clients need to clarify their respective and joint responsibilities. A non-exhaustive list might look like the following:

1. *Joint development of an understanding of the strategic and operational situations (positions) of brands and products.* Advertisers and agencies must develop a shared, equal and transparent understanding of the current strategic and operational situation of the advertisers' brands and products. These strategic and operational situations define the starting point for marketing performance improvement programs.

Advertisers need to involve agencies in the development of brand marketing analyses and plans, and to share, on an ongoing basis, the content of their final brand strategic and operational plans. It is within these documents that advertisers document and communicate to *their top manage-*

ment what their brand situations are and how management intends to work its way out of them through investments in marketing and sales. An unfortunate trend during the past decade has been "keeping agencies in the dark" and dealing with them at arm's length about a number of key things, like brand strategic analyses and operational plans. Today, this tendency manifests itself in a number of ways, like not sharing customer "big data" with ad agencies, either on the assumption that agencies cannot be trusted with this confidential data or that they are not sufficiently competent to use it and add value with it. The lack of trust is only understandable in an environment where advertisers change agencies with greater frequency and more whimsically than they did in the past. In our proposed scheme, agencies are changed only if there is a significant failure in the relationship, so the notion that confidential information cannot be exchanged is moot.

2. *Joint development of high-probability action plans for brands and products.* Advertisers and agencies must jointly develop and agree on proposed action plans for each brand and product. These proposed action plans should have, in the shared judgment of the advertiser and agency, the highest probability of delivering marketing success. The plans, of course, will need to be tried out in the marketplace and adjusted on the basis of market feedback and actual experience. Action plans can include the development of new products, new pricing strategies, expanded distribution, new messaging to consumers, revised media mixes, or a host of other marketing possibilities. *"What actions will best drive improved growth and profitability?"* ought to be the dominant question.

Key phrases, are "shared judgment" and "highest probability." Marketing involves an expenditure of today's dollars for an uncertain future outcome, just like any other business investment. How should marketing dollars be spent? What data, experience and judgment can be brought to bear to increase the odds of success? What is the expected outcome? On what key assumptions does an improved outcome rely? Advertisers and agencies bring different perspectives and skills when addressing these questions. Better that each party work with the other to resolve the uncertainties than for each to work independently, or even worse for the advertiser to work solo on the problem and then direct the agency to execute.[20]

3. *Joint development of relevant SOWs for brand action plans.* Advertisers, of course, ultimately approve and fund fiscal year SOWs involving media costs, agency fees and production budgets. Their own budgetary processes require them to do this *before* the beginning of their fiscal year – in October and November for fiscal years that begin on January 1, for example. All too often, agency fee and production budgets are determined by advertisers *before* detailed SOW campaigns and deliverables are planned for the year. Detailed SOW planning is completed *after-the-fact*, tailored to fit the advertiser's agreed budget figures, rather than the other way around. Agencies complain, nearly half-way through a fiscal year that *"we have still not signed a contract with the client, and it's already May!"* This is not because there are no client budgets. The budgets exist. The unsigned contracts are a symptom that the SOWs have not been planned in detail – they're being handled on an ad hoc basis. The agency is supposed to show its flexibility by reacting to any and all SOW initiatives as they come up. The result is unfunded scope creep, workloads that stretch agency resources, agency resentment and below-standard creative work.

These are not circumstances that drive the development of high-quality SOWs or, for that matter, high-quality relationships. Ad hoc SOW planning puts an advertiser in a dominant, 'superior' position and its agency in a submissive, victim-like role. The resulting work is less effective than it could be, and resentments build up in both parties. Agencies in this situation await the day when their clients will "finally get their act together," but they wait in vain.

Instead, agencies need to play an active role and work on an early, joint basis to propose SOWs that they believe will make a difference to brand performance. The time to do this is long before advertisers begin their internal budgeting deliberations over media costs, agency fees and production costs. To do this well requires agency sophistication and in-depth understanding of the client's brands' competitive and market-place dynamics, derived from an immersion in consumer, market and competitive data. It's the kind of analysis that used to be done routinely by senior agency client service executives during the media-commission days, when the clear market imperative was increased media spend – clients who outspent their competitors saw increased sales and market share gains. Since then, though, as the marketplace has become significantly more complicated and the commission system dropped, agency account executives have ironically retreated into more passive "servicing roles," and their analytical capabilities have withered on the vine. Analytical and planning capabilities can and must be rekindled.

The principles of a relationship document ought to specify that agencies be responsible for proposing relevant annual SOW deliverables for an agreed media mix. The SOW should be first prepared on a budget-blind basis, as if there were no realistic budget constraints – the focus should be more on "what kind of returns might we expect if we carried out this proposed SOW at this proposed cost." The proposed SOW should be designed to "implement the agreed action plans" through carefully-tailored mixes of marketing communications deliverables across media disciplines. Later, if budget constraints require a more modest program, the SOW can be cut down to size.

4. *Calculating agency staffing and fees for SOWs.* Agencies should propose appropriate, skilled and sufficient staffing headcounts and seniority mixes by department for the proposed SOWs, using agreed and transparent "resource standards" for each type of project in the SOWs, taking into account the total volume of work proposed. SMUs must be the key driver of agency resources on the basis of clear, transparent and jointly-agreed metrics.

Once agency resources are proposed, appropriate fees can be calculated.

Determining agency headcounts and fees from SOWs turns on its head the current practice where clients first establish agency fees and thus dictate agency headcounts without first establishing the quantity and type of work to be done. This practice, as we showed with The Daedalus Agency, sees agencies "staffing to fee" rather than "staffing to workloads," leaving them with inadequate resources to handle growing workloads.

5. *Tracking SOW adjustments throughout the year.* SOWs will be adjusted during the year as advertisers and their agencies receive market feedback and adjust and optimize marketing communications to improve results. The greater proportion of digital marketing in the SOW mix should put SOW development on a more experimental basis. Even though a great deal of thought may have gone into the original SOW planning, the marketplace harbors mysteries and uncertainty, as consumers themselves adjust and evolve their purchasing behavior in line with the evolution of new marketing technologies. The marketplace needs to be learned and relearned as it evolves. Social and mobile marketing are, at this time of writing, still relatively unproven, but with the passage of time, increased effectiveness can surely be expected. Increased experimentation across all marketing technologies will yield insights into what works best, and SOW development will become an ongoing process of planning, measuring and adjusting.

SOW changes will need to be tracked and measured, and the associated changes in agency resources and fees can then be made on a regular (say quarterly) basis. New deliverables will be added or changed; selected planned deliverables can be dropped. SOWs can be handled in a very dynamic way without changing overall fee budgets if the sum of all added and changed work is matched by the sum of all cancelled or dropped work. The more robust the tracking and measuring process, the more dynamic this process can be.

What inhibits experimentation today, at least from an agency perspective, is the underlying belief that SOW changes are synonymous with unpaid scope creep, which is detrimental for agency performance. Agencies will be unenthusiastic and passive participants in the SOW-experiment game as long as they feel as that they are carrying the costs and receiving no benefits. By contrast, the joint use of a robust SOW tracking system brings courage and commitment to SOW experimentation, and agencies, rather than passively resisting experimentation, can become enthusiastic participants.

6. *Eliminating process inefficiencies and non-value-added costs.* Both parties must commit to running a lean and efficient relationship with a minimum of unnecessary rebriefing, rework and other related inefficiencies that raise costs and undermine the ability of the relationship to perform as required to deliver improved results. Metrics like "mutually acceptable rework rates" and "number of ideas to be generated (for this type of brief)" and "number of creative teams to be used" need to be developed, agreed and used to measure relationship efficiencies on an ongoing basis.

Often, the source of process inefficiencies lies with the advertiser, who may have poor briefing and hierarchical ad approval processes. Poor briefings lead to off-brief work and rework; hierarchical ad approval processes involve delays and high levels of rework as each "approver" up the chain of command adds individual changes to submitted creative work. High rework rates, of course, add a creative burden to already-stretched agency creative resources and, in the end, foster lower rather than higher creative quality.

Procurement departments understand, in general, the deleterious effects of process inefficiencies, and in their usual professional dealings with manufacturing and distribution suppliers, they work diligently to eliminate inefficiencies. Somehow, though, this particular discipline did not migrate to advertiser-agency relationships when procurement first became involved, and both advertisers and agencies continued to live with one another in a way that tolerated if not exalted the reworking and continued reworking of creative work to "get it right." As laudatory as it is to be committed to overworking creative work until it is "exactly right," how much better to be committed to "getting it right and approved as soon as possible" and have an open dialogue with advertisers about what is required to bring this about.

Procurement departments, instead of investing in an effort to understand the "advertising process" and finding ways to eliminate relationship waste, fall back on pure fee-cutting, on the assumption that if agencies have less in the way of fees, agencies themselves will find ways to become more efficient. What this ignores, though, are two things: 1) agencies are absolutely terrible at managing their own processes, having no leadership, experience or capabilities to do so, and 2) the existence of briefing and ad approval process inefficiencies within advertisers' own marketing departments, which are invisible because SOW deliverables are not documented, tracked or measured. Fee-cutting does not reduce process inefficiencies; instead, it simply stretches resources further as workloads grow.

Briefing and ad approval inefficiencies are not the only inefficiencies that exist. Most agency contracts are written as labor-based contracts, which means that fees are calculated on the basis of a certain number of agreed agency man-hours for the fiscal year. In fact, agency man-hours are what advertisers are contractually buying rather than brand strategic studies and advertisements. As a reflection of this, many if not most advertiser-agency contracts are written as "reconcilable contracts," meaning that agency man-hours are audited, usually by the advertisers' internal audit departments, and if agencies deliver *fewer* man-hours than contracted, for whatever reason, they have to refund a portion of their fees; if agencies deliver *more* man-hours than contracted, they are entitled to more fees. This latter case is often not respected, though, since advertisers often argue that time sheet hour overage is simply due to agency "inefficiency." The agency process of delivering correct time sheet information and justifying overages or underages is extremely time-consuming for both parties. In the end, no one is satisfied with the results, because the principal argument, *"we did more/less work than forecasted"* falls on deaf ears when there are no specific workload measures.

The auditing of time sheet hours is a time wasting process that can be eliminated if contracts focus on paying agencies for deliverables rather than for man-hours.

7. *Mutual support of the relationship.* A relationship focused on achieving re-
    sults requires strong leadership from both parties. Relationships of this
    nature are negotiated at very high organizational levels, but the troops
    below the generals don't always get the word, and it is a normal feature
    of organizational life that junior people on both sides of the divide find
    ways to engage in conflicts and torture one another in minor and an-
    noying ways. Leadership is required to ensure that petty conflicts or the
    pursuit of selfish interests from within their respective organizations are
    not permitted to interfere or sabotage the joint aspirations and goals of
    the relationship.

    Within advertisers, this will require a balancing of the sometimes-com-
    peting interests of marketing and procurement, on the one hand, and
    between corporate marketing and local marketing organizations, on the
    other hand. The competing interests of marketing and procurement are
    easy to identify – marketing wants agencies to do more work at no extra
    cost, and procurement wants agencies' fees cut on a regular basis. Part of
    what has made advertiser-agency relationships increasingly dysfunction-
    al over time has stemmed from this dynamic, which has led to agencies
    doing more work for less money with fewer resources. The resentment
    that this generates is incompatible with the needs of a performance-fo-
    cused relationship. Marketing and procurement need to eliminate their
    inherent conflicts by changing the way agency contracts are structured,
    focusing on deliverables rather than hours.

    The competing interests of corporate marketing and local marketing
    are of an entirely different nature, but they can severely sabotage the re-
    sults-focused relationship. The conflict is over relative power. The type
    of advertiser-agency relationship we envision puts relatively more power
    in the hands of central marketing departments, since they have a larger
    say over agency SOWs, particularly for global relationships, and in global
    relationships this means "*more originations developed in the center (rather
    than locally), with adaptations handled locally.*" The relative power of local
    marketing organizations to direct agency ad origination is diminished,
    inevitably. In the worst of cases, local marketing organizations refuse to

play under the new rules, insisting on their right to direct local agency operations and to ignore centrally-generated advertising work that they do not feel is appropriate for their markets. Local agencies are all too willing to get sucked into this power-play, since they have many of the same resentments about being consigned to second-rate status by the agency center. There are few compromises that can satisfy the bruised egos that are created when the center takes more responsibility and power. Corporate and agency senior leaders must clearly communicate to their local operations that there is a new way of playing the game, and that instances of non-compliance will not be tolerated. Eventually, the new roles will become the old rules, and a new equilibrium can be established.

Agencies have built-in conflicts of their own. Agencies are organizationally a federation of individual profit-center offices rather than a portfolio of clients that happen to be served by multiple offices. Office heads and office finance directors seek to maximize office profit margins as a first priority; being "good global client providers" is further down the list. Offices understandably find it hard to make financial sacrifices for global clients that they merely service rather than run. Within agencies, leadership is required to ensure that the sometimes-selfish profit-center motives and behaviors of individual offices within the network are subordinated to the needs and interests of results-focused relationships. Strong leadership from agency CEOs on this issue needs to be made for the record and reinforced on an ongoing basis.

Finally, the senior leaders of advertisers and agencies have a responsibility to ensure the success of one another in their joint efforts to make these types of relationships a success. Conflicts must be smoothed out; junior executives and local organizations must be brought into line; procurement and marketing must find a way to work together to ensure relationship efficiency and fair compensation; and agencies must focus their creative efforts on advertising that works in the marketplace for the benefit of their clients.

CHAPTER 11 – MEASUREMENT OF SCOPES OF WORK

A Critique of Pure Reason

Credit: Paul Noth / The New Yorker / The Cartoon Bank.

I have not yet discussed where SMUs come from – how they were developed in the first place, and how agencies and advertisers can use them on their own to develop SOW management disciplines and create improved relationships.

HISTORY

My first ad agency consulting assignment was in 1992, when Farmer & Company was asked, in its capacity as a strategy consulting firm, to help determine why Tea & Crumpets UK (T&C), the London office of a (disguised name) major global advertising agency, had rather suddenly become unprofitable. The CEO responded to the profit problem with a number of extraordinary steps, including moving T&C's office to a new, low-cost location, while reducing overheads and freezing salaries and bonuses. Still, operating margins hovered at 5%, which was then half of the desired level. Something in T&C's internal operations was awry, and the CEO thought that a strategy consultant might help to uncover the reasons.

After some initial interviews and a review of industry and agency data, we learned that our client had enjoyed a long period of media price inflation from about 1975 to 1990, and that the increased revenues from inflating media prices allowed the office to invest in additional costs to provide increased services for clients, like strategic planning and research services – in the hope that these increased services would somewhat mollify client resentment over the "free revenue ride" the agency enjoyed from media price inflation.

By 1990, fee-based remuneration was replacing media commissions, and this drove revenue downwards. Logically, T&C's managing director could have reduced costs and services at a fast rate to match the reductions in revenue, but he found that cost and service *reductions* were a lot harder to implement than cost and service *increases* – services for clients could not simply be turned off like a faucet. Furthermore, he was not sure that his problem was chronic and long term. He did not want to take draconian cost reduction steps at a time when his profit problem might disappear as mysteriously as it appeared. Consequently, the steps he took to reduce costs and services lagged his revenue reductions, and office margins were squeezed.

This was our hypothesis about the situation, and in graphic form it looked like Table 11-1, below.

TABLE 11-1: THE CHANGING PRICE AND COST PATTERNS

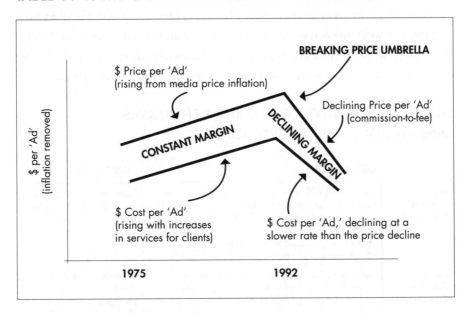

This generic pattern of price and cost behavior had been characterized as the *"breaking price umbrella"* by The Boston Consulting Group in one of Bruce Henderson's "Perspectives" in 1968.[21]

If our hypothesis was right – that this was an example of a breaking price umbrella – then T&C had few remedies other than accelerated cost reduction. The challenge would be to determine how this could be done without crippling agency operations.

The hypothesis could be verified if the right price and cost data could be gathered and analyzed. The *right data*, though, was *unit price data (price per ad)* and *unit cost data (cost per ad)*, and this required an understanding of the *number of units (number of ads)* being developed and produced by the agency. We couldn't simply count up the TV, radio and print ads for each year, since each type of ad was unique in its own way. A TV ad was not the same as a print ad in terms of the amount of work (man-hours) involved in its development and production. TV ads were "bigger" than print ads. In addition, each ad in each medium was either an original piece of work or an adaptation of previously developed work, and within these two categories there were at least three different levels of creative complexity (low, average and high) based on how original the work needed to be. High creative complexity ads were 100% original and took more time and used more creative resources than low creative complexity ads, which were based on ideas from existing ad campaigns.

TABLE 11-2: CREATIVE COMPLEXITY DEFINITIONS ORIGINATIONS AND ADAPTATIONS

	ORIGINATIONS	ADAPTATIONS
High Creative Complexity:	Associated with new strategic briefs, requiring many (3+) new creative routes as outlined in a new creative brief. Typically this is for a new product, a launch, a relaunch or a line extension. These could be characterized as "here's something entirely new and original."	Complete change to two-thirds of Script/Sound/Copy, Storyboard/Layout, or Footage/Image.
Average Creative Complexity:	Secondary/ongoing deliverables from an existing strategic brief, but involving a new creative brief requiring at least 1-2 creative routes. These could be characterized as "something new, but in line with what has been done previously."	Complete change to one-third, or minor changes to two-thirds of Script/Sound/Copy, Storyboard/Layout, or Footage/Image.
Low Creative Complexity:	These involve a single creative route, from an existing strategic and creative brief, with very little need for new creative thinking. These could be characterized as "more of the same, but different in some minor way."	Minor change to one-third of Script/ Sound/Copy, Storyboard/Layout, or Footage/Image.

At a very aggregate level, there were 18 traditional advertising brief types, as shown below in Table 11-3.

TABLE 11-3: EIGHTEEN MAJOR BRIEF TYPES – 1992 ABOVE-THE-LINE

MEDIA TYPE	ORIGINATION			ADAPTATION		
	Creative Complexity			Creative Complexity		
	Low	Average	High	Low	Average	High
TV	1	2	3	4	5	6
Print/Poster	7	8	9	10	11	12
Radio	13	14	15	16	17	18

However, this too, is an oversimplification, since there are "creative-only" briefs that have no production, "production-only" briefs whose creative development work is done elsewhere or earlier, and "full-up" briefs that include creative development and production. Those additional three categories take the total inventory of briefs up to 54 types. Even this oversimplifies the situation, since within the print/poster category there are a number of different types of ads, including black-and-white newspaper ads, full-color magazine ads, outdoor billboards, catalogues, brochures, fliers, Sunday free-standing inserts, and dozens of others. There were, in addition, multimedia ads, like TV plus print, and TV plus print plus radio which were not simply the sum of their constituent parts.

We needed to find a way to develop a "unifying workload metric" for this highly diverse mix of briefs. We reasoned that it was like trying to evaluate a basket of fruit containing a number and mix of fruits. How could you evaluate it so that you could compare it to another basket of fruits? You'd have to find a "unifying metric," like *weight* (you'd weigh and compare the baskets) or *caloric content* (using weight and caloric values per ounce or gram for each type of fruit, and then comparing the calories per basket).

SOWs presented us with the same type of problem. Let's say, for example, that one client in T&C had a SOW with a mix of 50 various TV and radio briefs, and another client had a mix of 75 print ads. Which advertiser had the larger SOW? Which advertiser required the greater number of creative and production resources? By how much? It was not possible to know by simply counting the briefs.

We reasoned that *creative man-hours* for each type of brief *at a standard level of resource*, which we defined as *one creative team, with zero rework*, would be like *weight* or *caloric value* for a basket of fruit.

The use of creative man-hours for each type of ad would allow us standardize SOWs across T&C's clients and arrive at a unit price (fee divided by workload) and unit cost (cost divided by workload). Once we had this, then we could analyze and diagnose T&C's price and cost behavior.

Determining the creative man-hours was not our first challenge, though. The first challenge was to gather SOWs – the list of ads developed and produced for each client, classified by media type, origination/adaptation and by creative complexity. We hoped to be able to identify which of these briefs used multiple creative teams during creative development, and how many rounds of rework each brief went through before being approved for production by the client.

We were disappointed to discover that the T&C client heads did not keep track of the work they did for each of their clients, much less know how many creative teams were involved or what the rework rates were. They knew, in a general way, what work they had done, but it required an effort to document it in writing. T&C, like other agency offices (we later learned), simply did not worry about documenting or tracking the work they completed, at least not in a way that was convenient or structured. Workload was not perceived as an important factor in the management of agency operations. No one asked for workloads by client or reviewed changes in workload from one year to another. There was no master list of completed ads in a prominent file on someone's desk – or, for that matter, hidden away somewhere in a desk drawer. The historical record of work was scattered throughout the T&C organization in various filing cabinets and in the heads of those whose memories were good. Files of T&C job invoices (bills from photographers, invoices from production companies, travel receipts, etc.) were kept in "job jackets" in finance and production, used for the preparation of expense reimbursement invoices for clients. Weekly lists of current briefs were kept separately on Excel sheets for T&C's Monday morning meetings, which were conducted every week to review jobs-in-process. But nowhere were the data we sought to understand the amount of client-by-client workload from one year to another, and how much creative resource they used and how much rework they incurred. Timesheet records, we found, were nearly useless for this purpose, since job numbers were not aligned with creative deliverables or even (in some cases) with client brands. Some accounts were assigned one single job number to capture all agency hours.

We abandoned our quest to construct a multi-year record of T&C's price and cost history, and instead we concentrated on gathering the 1991 and 1992 SOWs through a forensic and interview-based process, digging through job jackets and interviewing client service executives (65 in number), strategic planners (10), creatives (52) and production people (40) to reconstruct the most recent SOWs. This took several weeks. Our plan was to build a database of T&C's creative briefs, with the actual number of creative teams used on each brief and the actual rework rates incurred by brief, to be called the "T&C actual brief database" – and then work with the creatives to develop what we called "T&C creative day standards" to answer the following question:

- For each type of brief (*by media type, by origination / adaptation, by creative complexity*), working under ideal productivity circumstances (*no exceptional internal delays or client-driven rework delays*), how many full working days would it take one creative team, on average, to do the following:

  1. *Creative days in creative development.* Complete the creative development work on each type of brief, including reviewing the work internally and then with the client to gain client approval, *and*

2. *Creative days in production.* Oversee each brief's creative content through the production process to the air/insertion date.

We reasoned that once we had the T&C actual brief database and T&C creative day standards for each type of brief, we could use these two sources of data to calculate the *actual number of creatives required* for the T&C SOWs. This ought to come very close to the *actual number of creatives in the T&C office working at standard billability.* After sick days and holidays, standard billability (utilization) was 86.5%, or 225 working days (1,800 hours) per creative during the year. Thus, 52 creatives or 26 creative teams ought to complete 11,700 creative days (93,600 billable hours) working on creative deliverables.

If our T&C actual brief database was correct (there were 363 various briefs), and the T&C creative day standards for each type of brief were accurate as well, then if we multiplied each actual brief by its appropriate creative day standard and summed up the total for all of the briefs, we would have total creative team-days required for the office's SOWs, taking into account the usage of multiple teams and the actual rework rates.

It took a number of iterations to micro-adjust each of the T&C creative day standards so that their final values would generate 11,700 creative days for 52 creatives from the 363 briefs in the T&C actual brief database, but after some careful adjustments, we found the right set of values, which are shown below.

TABLE 11-4: FINAL T&C CREATIVE DAY STANDARDS 1992

CREATIVE TIME IN CREATIVE DEVELOPMENT						
One team, no reworks	MAN-DAYS PER TEAM			MAN-DAYS PER TEAM		
	For an Origination by Complexity			For an Adaptation by Complexity		
	Low	Average	High	Low	Average	High
TV/Cinema	7.0	11.2	16.4	2.3	3.8	5.2
TV/Cinema/Print	10.5	15.5	21.6	3.6	5.5	7.3
Print/Poster	5.4	9.0	13.3	1.7	2.8	4.1
Radio alone	6.0	8.0	13.0	2.5	3.5	5.5
Radio additional	1.7	2.3	4.0	1.0	1.5	3.0

CREATIVE TIME IN PRODUCTION		
One team, average production rework	MAN-DAYS PER TEAM	MAN-DAYS PER TEAM
	For an Origination	For an Adaptation
	For all Creative Complexities	For all Creative Complexities
TV/Cinema	10.8	3.0
TV/Cinema/Print	14.4	4.0
Print/Poster	5.2	1.2
Radio alone	11.0	1.6
Radio additional	2.5	1.6

Sample calculation. Let's go through a sample calculation, using a single brief, to show how the system worked. Table 11-5 shows a highly contentious and inefficient brief that the agency described to us as an "out-of-control" brief:

TABLE 11-5: AN AUTOMOTIVE BRIEF IN THE T&C ACTUAL BRIEF DATABASE 1991

CLIENT	AUTOMOTIVE
Name of Brief	New model launch 1992
Media Type	Multimedia: TV/Print
Brief Type	Origination
Creative Complexity	High
Actual Number of Creative Teams Used in Creative Development	4
Actual Rework Rate	5
CREATIVE DAY STANDARD: Creative Team-Days in Creative Development for this type of brief (for one team, no rework)	21.6
CREATIVE DAY STANDARD: Creative Team-Days in Production for this type of brief (for one team, average production rework)	14.4

The T&C client was an automotive company that represented a very import-ant percentage of the office's income. The brief was for a multimedia TV and print ad for a new car model launch in 1992 – launches took place every four years or so, and they were very big marketing events. The client was looking for an exceptionally large number of creative "big ideas" for the vehicle, which was a smaller and more fuel-efficient vehicle. The agency was under pressure to show a wide range of creative ideas and, once the ideas were winnowed down, to produce and air brilliant campaigns.

The two executive creative directors assigned an exceptional number of cre-ative teams to this brief – four full teams (one copywriter and one art director each) – and the four teams were directed to generate eight unique campaign ideas, each of which was subsequently reviewed by the executive creative di-rectors. The executive creative directors wanted to "wow" the client with the agency's creative capabilities. Of the eight big ideas, six were selected for presentation to the client at the first major creative review. This began a process that saw, as a result of the review, two creative ideas out of the six earmarked for further development for TV and print, the four creative teams reduced to one "winning" team, and five full rounds of additional rework incurred by the winning team over the next several weeks. Subsequently, after a number of additional reviews with the client, the final campaign was approved and put into production, and the winning creative team saw the brief through the production process. A further number of TV, print and radio campaigns based on the winning idea were developed subsequently over the course of the year.

Rework, as described above, was defined as "an amount of additional creative time equal to the original creative development time spent by one creative team." Normally, there are three to four "tweaks" per rework, so for the five full reworks, there were about 15 and 20 changes in the brief, directed by the client as the brief wound its way slowly through the ad approval process.

In sum, the brief went through one creative development process with each of the four creative teams, so there were effectively four creative development cycles, plus five full rounds of rework with the one winning creative team. This means that the brief had the equivalent of nine full cycles of creative development – four during creative idea development, and five during creative idea refinement – before the brief was finally approved by the client and could begin to be produced.

Summary of one brief. Nine creative development cycles at 21.6 creative team-days each equaled 194.4 creative team-days for creative development. There were an additional 14.4 creative team-days in production, so the total creative effort took 208.8 creative team-days, or 417.6 creative man-days, or 3,340.8 creative man-hours (at eight hours per day). This was equivalent to using 1.86 creative full-time equivalents (FTEs) for the year (3,340.8 hours ÷ 1,800 hours).

Summary of the office. For the 363 briefs completed during the year, according to our analysis, the *average* number of creative teams per brief was 2.3 (varying from a high of six teams per brief to a low of 0.5 teams per brief), and the *average* number of full reworks was 2.6 reworks per brief. This was an exceptionally high number of average creative teams per brief and rework rates across the SOW. The T&C CEO was upset with the way the two executive creative directors were lavishly allocating creative teams to the office's work. "*Here we are,*" he said, "*struggling to make a profit, and the creative directors are acting as if creative resources are unlimited and free. No wonder they keep asking for more people! They are totally undisciplined and out of touch with our financial situation.*"

A more efficient scenario. The CEO asked us to model a more efficient scenario, using the actual briefs and seeing how many creatives would be required if creative resources were allocated in a different way. We established, with the input of various people in the agency, what came to be called "T&C Gold Resource Standards" that had the following structure:

TABLE 11-6: AGREED T&C GOLD RESOURCE STANDARDS FOR CREATIVE TEAM ASSIGNMENTS 1992

	GOLD RESOURCE STANDARDS					
	ORIGINATIONS			ADAPTATIONS		
	Low	Average	High	Low	Average	High
Number of Creative Teams	1	1	2	0.5	0.5	0.5
Expected Rework Rate	0.5	1	2	0.25	0.5	0.5

No brief was expected to be given more than two creative teams and to incur more than two rounds of rework. The *typical* brief would have about one creative team (or less, for adaptations) and about one rework or less.

Let's see the effect of the T&C gold resource standards on the multimedia automotive brief, which had taken 1.86 creative FTEs as a result of the assignment of four creative teams and a rework rate of five full reworks. If the same brief had been handled according to T&C gold resource standards, the brief would have had two creative teams and incurred two full reworks:

TABLE 11-7: AN AUTOMOTIVE BRIEF IF STAFFED AT T&C GOLD RESOURCE STANDARDS

CLIENT	AUTOMOTIVE
Name of Brief	New model launch 1992
Media Type	Multimedia: TV/Print
Brief Type	Origination
Creative Complexity	High
Gold Number of Creative Teams Used in Creative Development	2
Gold Rework Rate	2
CREATIVE DAY STANDARD: Creative Team-Days in Creative Development for this type of brief (for one team, no rework)	21.6
CREATIVE DAY STANDARD: Creative Team-Days in Production for this type of brief (for one team, average production rework)	14.4

Summary of one brief at T&C gold resource standards. Four creative development cycles (1 for each team plus two reworks) at 21.6 creative team-days each equaled 86.4 creative team-days for creative development. There were an additional 14.4 creative team-days in production, so the total creative effort took 100.8 creative team-days, or 201.6 creative man-days, or 1,612.8 creative man-hours (at eight hours per day). This was equivalent to the use of 0.90 creative FTEs for the year (1,612.8 hours divided by 1,800 hours).

At T&C gold resource standards, this brief took 0.90 creative FTEs rather than 1.86 creative FTEs, or fewer than half of the actual creatives assigned.

We modeled the office's 363 briefs on this basis, and instead of requiring 52 total creatives (at an average of 2.3 teams per brief with 2.6 average reworks per brief) the new T&C gold standard allocation required 35 creatives (at an average of 1 team per brief and 1 reworks per brief). This was a third less than the current creative staffing. Furthermore, the expected reduction in coordination activities associated with creative reviews and rework at the client could lead to a reduction in client service personnel from 65 FTEs to 44 FTEs while maintaining a ratio of 1.25 client service FTEs per creative FTE.

Our SOW analysis and subsequent discussions at T&C concluded with the following summary:

- *T&C profitability was depressed by a 30% over-allocation of creative resources across the SOW, on the one hand, and the provision of a large number of client service personnel to handle the high coordination needs associated with high rates of rebriefing, reviews and rework.*

- *While this level of over-allocation of resources might have made sense and was affordable during the media commission days, it was no longer affordable in the expectation of further fee cuts in a fee-based environment. New rules for the allocation of resources needed to be established and used.*

- *A more rational allocation of creative resources, using T&C gold resource standards to limit creative teams to one creative team per brief (except for high creative complexity briefs), leading to fewer client reviews and lower rework rates, would not only reduce creative costs but also permit a reduction in client service staffing.*

T&C took on board these advised recommendations and then proceeded as follows for 1993:

1. Every client head was required to forecast his/her 1993 SOW, using "Farmer format:" Media type, origination/adaptation and creative complexity (low, average, high).

2. The SOWs were modeled, using T&C gold resource standards, to determine the appropriate gold standard creative staffing for each client.

3. The CEO and his executive team conducted "live SOW reviews" with each client head, reviewing the proposed SOWs for each client and ensuring that the client head understood and accepted the revised creative staffing on his/her account.

4. The creative staffing for all accounts was summed up, and an additional 10% headcount cushion was added for new business and other contingencies, leading to a proposed T&C creative staffing level of 39 creative FTEs, down from 52 creatives during 1992. Client service headcounts were similarly reduced, to 49 FTEs, down from 65 during 1992.

5. The two executive creative directors, whose management of creative staffing was partly responsible for the office's profit problem, decided to resign rather than work under more tightly managed circumstances, and they were replaced by a new executive creative director who was prepared to work with the CEO to improve creative quality within the more tightly-managed creative capacity constraints at the same time.

6. The T&C profit margin increased from 5% to 14% in 1993, and the new SOW forecasting and management system was adapted on a permanent basis.

This work for T&C identified a cost management problem that was depressing profitability – creative costs were being managed according to old rules developed during the more lavish media commission era. The need for a more stringent resource management approach was not recognized until profits were at a very depressed level. Measurement of workload and the adoption of new resource management standards were required.

Over the next decade, until 2003, Farmer & Company worked with T&C's offices and with other global advertising agencies, taking our SOW analyses from one office to another. We reconstructed traditional advertising SOWs (TV, radio, print), documented the number and type of briefs, determined the number of creative teams and the actual rework rates by brief, modeled the actual brief databases and found over-allocations of creative and client service resources. The problem seemed endemic at the 30 agency offices we diagnosed over this 10-year period. Our findings were certainly consistent with the existence of breaking price umbrellas and lagging cost management practices. Routinely, we found surplus creative and client service resources that accounted for the depressed profitability that agency offices were experiencing between 1993 and 2003.

We were reassured that our traditional advertising SOW resource model seemed to work well in different agency offices in the US, Europe and Asia – accurately calculating the number of actual creatives in an office from the actual brief databases and the creative day standards. Ad agencies, we learned, worked in the same way around the world, taking the same amount of time per creative team to develop and produce ads. Agency offices varied from one another only in the degree to which they used multiple creative teams and incurred rework – and in the salary levels they paid their people. Agency offices were otherwise uniform in the way they used creative resources for the basic business of creating and producing traditional ads.

THE SCOPEMETRIC® UNIT (SMU)

We reasoned that a standardized unit of work for a SOW could be based on creative man-hours for a given creative deliverable at an appropriate level of creative staffing and productivity. A TV origination ad of high creative complexity could be valued at X units of work (based on the creative man-hours required for two creative teams and two reworks for this category of ad) while a TV adaptation ad of low creative complexity could be valued at Y units of work (based on 0.5 creative teams and 0.25 reworks for this category of ad).

The unit of work needed to be simple and easy to communicate. I remembered something David Ogilvy wrote about creative productivity in *Ogilvy* on Advertising: "*The average copywriter gets only three commercials a year on air.*" (Ogilvy, 1983, p. 20).

If creative productivity for traditional advertising had improved modestly by (say) 1.5% per year since David Ogilvy's 1983 assertion of three commercials per creative, then by 2003 the "*average creative would complete to 4.1 ads per year.*"

If we modeled all types of creative deliverables, one at a time, using our proven creative day standards and gold resource standards, then our resource model would tell us how many creative FTEs would be required to take each deliverable through creative development and production.

TABLE 11-8: CREATIVE FTES AT GOLD RESOURCE STANDARDS FOR A SELECTION OF BRIEF TYPES (CREATIVE FTE = 1,800 HOURS)

	LOW CREATIVE COMPLEXITY	AVERAGE CREATIVE COMPLEXITY	HIGH CREATIVE COMPLEXITY
FULL-UP ORIGINATIONS	Creative FTEs Rounded	Creative FTEs Rounded	Creative FTEs Rounded
TV/Cinema	0.10	0.15	0.35
Print/Poster	0.06	0.11	0.27
Radio	0.08	0.10	0.23
ADAPTATIONS			
TV/Cinema	0.02	0.03	0.04
Print/Poster	0.01	0.02	0.02
Radio	0.01	0.02	0.03

If we took these FTE values and multiplied them by 4.1 then we would have SMU values for this sample of briefs:

TABLE 11-9: SMU VALUES FOR A SELECTION OF BRIEF TYPES (BASED ON A CREATIVE PRODUCTIVITY LEVEL OF 4.1 SMUS PER CREATIVE PER YEAR)

	LOW CREATIVE COMPLEXITY	AVERAGE CREATIVE COMPLEXITY	HIGH CREATIVE COMPLEXITY
FULL-UP ORIGINATIONS	SMUs	SMUs	SMUs
TV/Cinema	0.40	0.62	1.43
Print/Poster	0.25	0.43	1.09
Radio	0.32	0.43	0.93
ADAPTATIONS			
TV/Cinema	0.09	0.13	0.15
Print/Poster	0.05	0.07	0.10
Radio	0.05	0.08	0.11

A number of key generalizations can be made from the simple SMU table above:

- High complexity originations are about 2.3 times as large as average complexity originations;
- Average complexity originations are about 1.5 times as large as low complexity originations;
- Adaptations, in general, are between 1/5th and 1/10th the size of comparable originations.

In 2004, once we developed the SMU, we set about to gather and create SMU values for briefs in direct marketing and digital media. We were fortunate in this respect, because we were working with a number of direct marketing and digital agencies whose SOWs were in these areas, and they had a keen interest in developing workload and resource values, using our methodology.

By 2007, we had 2,749 different types of briefs in our SMU database. The SMU database became a unique analytical resource, permitting us to determine how much work was involved in any given SOW. The briefs covered a wide range of areas – see below.

TABLE 11-10: SOW BRIEF CATEGORIES AND NUMBER OF BRIEF TYPES

Farmer SOW Metrics	Number of Projects in Category
Ad Unit - Banners	62
Applications	108
Digital Online Mktg	30
Email - eDM	35
Event Radio	12
Event TV	72
Healthcare Professional	39
Online Videos	225
OOH	393
Print - DM	144
Print - Non-Traditional	405
Print - Traditional	153
Radio	186
Social Media	81
TV	405
Video	261
Website	138
TOTAL	**2,749**

Many of the briefs in this database were relatively similar to one another. For example, the TV category had 405 distinct SMU values, as shown above. This was due to having 34 TV project definitions that we came across during our work (shown on the next page in Table 11-11), and each of these was further categorized as a 1) full-up origination, or 2) creative only origination, or 3) production only origination, or 4) adaptation, with 5) low creative complexity, or 6) average creative complexity or 7) high creative complexity. Each of these brief categories had slightly different SMU values for the 34 different project definitions.

TABLE 11-11: 34 TV PROJECT CATEGORIES
IN THE SOW DATABASE

Animated Billboard	TV :10	TV :25/:05
Cross Channel Promo :15	TV :120	TV :30
Cross Channel Promo :30	TV :15	TV :30/:15
Cross Channel Promo :60	TV :20	TV :40
Electronic Billboard	TV :23	TV :45
In Office Spot - TV	TV :28	TV :60
Other - See Comments	TV :15/:20	TV :75
Script/Live Read	TV :25/:28	TV :90
Test commercial	Testing	TV Footer Ad
TV Transadaptation	Shadow Shoot	TV Tag
TV :05	TV :20/:05	
TV :07	TV :25	

Armed with the SMU, we revisited the SOWs and resource plans of all our clients since 1992. We were interested in answering two questions:

What was the Price per SMU paid to our clients for their SOWs? Price was defined as fee income divided by workload in SMUs. We removed inflation by using published GDP deflators, and we used the then-current exchange rates so that our analysis would be in constant dollars.

What was the creative productivity over time, and how had it changed? Creative productivity was total number of SMUs per year divided by the number of creative FTEs.

We have shown in previous chapters the two displays that answer these questions, but it is instructive to repeat them here.

TABLE 11-12: PRICE CURVE 1992-2014
(PRICES IN $2014 PER SMU)

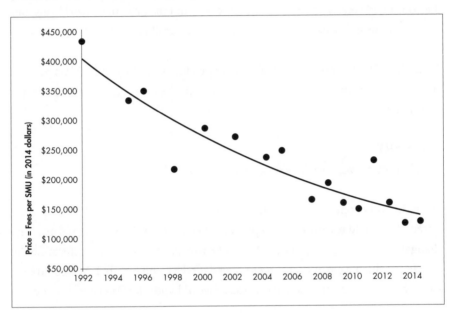

Source: Farmer & Company client data

TABLE 11-13: INCREASE IN CREATIVE PRODUCTIVITY
(1992-2012) (SMUS PER CREATIVE PER YEAR)

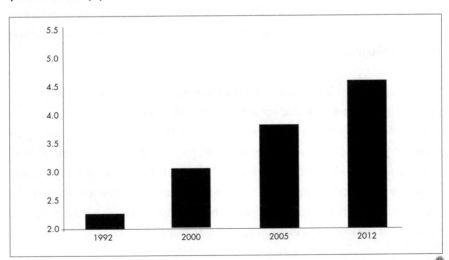

Creative productivity had been 2.3 SMUs per creative per year in 1992 for our clients, even less than the three ads per year described by David Ogilvy[22], but with the continued deterioration of client fee levels, and the growth of workloads, our clients had been downsizing and driving creative productivity levels upwards.

Today (2015), the average level of creative productivity is about 5 SMUs per creative, and it is rising. This is not a healthy trend. Creatives are being increasingly stretched.

SUMMARY

It took us many years to develop a database of workload values.

Once this was done, we had all the elements we needed for a SOW diagnostic system. We could review industry pricing behavior over time. We could examine changes in creative productivity. We could take apart a SOW and determine the degree to which agency clients were overstaffed or understaffed. We could pick apart the operations of an agency office, as we did with the Daedalus Agency.

We did all of these things over many years, and they told us a story about what was happening in the industry. Workloads were growing; fees were flat or declining; prices were falling; creative resources were being stretched – and these problems were continuing, principally because agencies were not documenting, tracking or negotiating their workloads with their clients. Management priorities were, instead, focused on new business development, although this was not solving the problem.

In the end, this "workload story" describes the unhappy circumstances that define agency life. The story has not yet come to an end, since each year brings greater workloads, lower prices and fewer resources, but the inevitable consequences can surely be predicted. Sooner or later, for one agency or many, the promised level of profit margins will not be generated, and this will affect holding company performance. The superior margins from media operations will no longer mask the weaker margins from ad agency operations, and embarrassing questions will be asked about the earnings quality of the holding company portfolio.

CHAPTER 12 – PRODUCTION, CLIENT SERVICE AND STRATEGIC PLANNING RESOURCES

Credit: Tom Cheney / The New Yorker / The Cartoon Bank.

The previous chapter described the origin and basis of the SMU and focused on the variability of creative resources and costs relative to workload. In fact, the variability is so predictable that we can use calculated creative resources (at gold resource standards) as the basis for defining the

SMU. Accordingly, we pegged the SMU as *"4.1 times calculated creative FTEs for a given creative deliverable (brief) at its relevant gold standard determined resource value."*

What about the other key resources, like production, client service and strategic planning? How do these resources vary with the work in agency SOWs? More to the point, how do these resources vary with the workload as defined by SMUs?

Broadly speaking, all agency resources are variable with workload. Creative, production, client service and strategic planning resources increase with increases in SMUs, and they decrease with decreases in SMUs. However, there are some additional unique factors that influence the degree of variability of these resources, and these unique factors must be taken into account when using SMUs to calculate resource requirements.

Let's look at the variability of resources, department by department.

PRODUCTION RESOURCES

As with creative resources, production resources vary directly with SMUs, but the variability of production resources is a function of the media type as well.

Certain types of media are more "production intensive" than other types of media. To illustrate, I've taken the Farmer & Company database of 2,749 brief types and looked at one uniform category: the 160 briefs that are classified as "full-up originations of average creative complexity among 10 selected media categories." For briefs in this uniform category, average production resources vary from a low of 0.104 FTEs per SMU (social media) to a high of 0.238 FTEs per SMU (online videos) within the 10 media types shown below in Table 12-1. That's more than a 2:1 difference in production intensity for a uniform type of brief that varies only by media.

TABLE 12-1: PRODUCTION FTES PER SMU FOR VARIOUS MEDIA TYPES

Media Type		Brief Classification	Number of Brief types in our database in this Classification	Average Number of Production FTEs per SMU in this Classification
1	Social Media	Origination, Full-up, Average Creative Complexity	7	0.104
2	Radio	Ditto	16	0.105
3	Email - eDM	Ditto	4	0.107
4	Ad Unit - Banners	Ditto	7	0.107
5	OOH	Ditto	33	0.123
6	Print - Traditional	Ditto	13	0.126
7	Digital Online Mktg	Ditto	5	0.154
8	TV	Ditto	34	0.164
9	Video	Ditto	22	0.238
10	Online Videos	Ditto	19	0.238
	Total		**160**	**0.159**

Media type and brief classification drive the production resources per SMU. If both are known, then with our SMU database, production resources can be determined easily, using an SMU and resource look-up table.

Within these media types as shown above, the weighted average production resource for full-up originations of average complexity, is 0.159 FTEs per SMU, or about 0.76 production FTEs per creative FTE. For a more typical mix of briefs across all media types and across all classifications (originations and adaptations of all creative complexities), the average production resource is about 0.14 production FTEs per SMU, or about 0.7 production FTEs per creative FTE. For a traditional-only mix of briefs, the average production resource is about 0.11 production FTEs per SMU, or about 0.55 production

FTEs per creative FTE. These are, of course, averages based on certain SOW mix assumptions rather than benchmarks that can be used in a general way.

The fact that digital briefs have a higher intensity of production resources than traditional briefs should be self-evident. For digital briefs, there is a substantial need for unique in-house production resources – software programmers, designers and technologists. The agency in-house production cost structure for digital work is a heavy one, indeed, particularly when the digital work involves website creation.

Ad agencies' traditional advertising in-house production resources include print producers for all print-related work and broadcast producers for radio and TV. All other production resources are bought in (photographers, production companies and so on) and paid for separately by advertisers through their production budgets. The proportion of traditional internal production resources versus bought-in production resources is relatively minor – exactly the opposite of digital production resources.

My friend and professional colleague Joe Burton, who was formerly chief operating officer for McCann's San Francisco operation, often had to explain the difference between digital and traditional agency costs to advertiser clients who assumed that "digital was less expensive than traditional" and tried to negotiate lower agency fees for digital work.

Partly out of frustration, Joe authored a guide that was later published by 4A's as *A Marketer's Guide to Understanding the Economics of Digital Compared to Traditional Advertising and Media Services* (Burton, 2009). One series of quotes from this informative publication succinctly makes the case for the higher production cost structure of digital advertising:

1. *"The ANA estimates that 74% of agency compensation arrangements are labor-based fees. However, advertisers still tend to think in terms of effective commission rates (especially when considering the overall price and reasonability of a particular program)."*

2. *"If traditional services are assumed to require staffing/fees that imply an effective commission rate in the range of 12-15% (with media planning and buying services assumed to be 1/4 of the total), digital can typically require resources that equate to an effective commission rate ranging from 25-30% (with media planning and buying services assumed to be half of the total)."*

3. *"Traditional media is generally understood to require a creative development process and a separate disciplined production process. For example, the great creative print idea is turned over to production for photo shoots, graphic design rough cuts, finishing touches and so on. Similarly, the broadcast production may involve the management of film shoots, directors, talent, talent rights, etc. Although the traditional process is managed by the agency, much of the actual production occurs through external third-party vendors. This is generally not the case for digital production."*

4. *"Unlike traditional efforts, much of the digital production process occurs in-house in real time with technical requirements often informing the creative idea. In order to keep pace with the marketplace (and to avoid putting themselves out of business), most agencies have had to develop the tools, technology and skills to handle digital creative development and production internally."* (Burton, 2009)

Armed with our database of production resources per SMU by media type, we can calculate an agency's need for production resources, based on a properly structured SOW as the input.

CLIENT SERVICE AND STRATEGIC PLANNING RESOURCES

Client service people have the responsibility to manage client relationships, to ensure that there are clear brand strategies to guide creative work, to handle the briefing of creative teams for new creative work, to handle the planning, coordination and approval of creative work at their clients (including coordinating rework), and to see that production work is done on time to meet media deadlines. When their clients are global clients, additional senior client service executives will oversee and coordinate SOW and resourcing activities on behalf of the client for several agency offices throughout the network. If the agency is a "brand navigator" or "brand account leader" or "integrator" of

a number of agencies for the client, then additional senior client service executives will be responsible for global brand strategies as well as SOW and resourcing issues on behalf of the client for these related or unrelated agencies.

In the name of client relationship management, client service executives provide ongoing services and hands-on help – by writing presentations for client
executives, completing competitive analyses, providing briefings, dealing with
budgetary and SOW changes, and generally doing everything they can to ensure that operations between the agency and the client run smoothly. Creating
good will is high on the list of any client service executive's priorities.

Brand strategic planning based on consumer insights was once exclusively in
the hands of senior client service executives, but the creation of the separate
strategic planning department with specialized strategic planners changed
this. Despite the existence of these specialists, though, brand strategic planning remains under the general executive responsibility of senior client service executives, so as a rule we think of client service and strategic planning as
a *single agency resource*. Hereinafter, I will refer to this single agency resource
as "CS&P resources" or "CS&P people."

Despite our best efforts over the years, we have been unable to directly model
an agency's need for CS&P resources based on the various activities that these
individuals engage in. That's because their activities are an absolute hodge-
podge of services that vary significantly by client and by circumstances. A list
of what CS&P people do on behalf of their clients would be staggeringly long,
and none of the services could be seen as uniform in any way. This stands in
direct contrast to the general uniformity of what agency creatives or production people do when making different types of ads.

Uniformity is not the case for CS&P people. More accurately, their work is
varied, and for them as for many others, "*work expands so as to fill the time
available for its completion*," in the memorable words of Cyril Northcote Parkinson.[23] For a given number of CS&P people, a unique mix of client services
will be carried out that consumes the billable capacity of the individuals. It's
probably fair to say that even if the number of individuals on a client account

were increased by (say) 50%, their collective client service work would expand by 50%, as well.

This phenomenon reminds me of a story told to me by John McArthur, Dean of Harvard Business School from 1980 to 1996.

"When I was the head of the MBA Program in the 1970s, our students seemed to think that their student life was uniquely stressful, and almost every week I had representatives from the Student Association in my office to complain about how tough it was and how unhappy students were and how wrong it was that we did not have sufficient counseling services to help them deal with the school. After listening to this for a while, I finally gave in and hired several more psychologists. They got started, and they were busy dealing with student issues, but somehow this did not quiet things down. Quite the opposite. The demand grew quickly in response to the supply. The Student Association was still outside my door with even more complaints, and now in addition it was impossible to get an appointment with the counseling service, and everyone was particularly unhappy. I looked into this, and it was true that the counselors were very busy. So we hired some more psychologists, and then even more. At one point I think we had around a dozen counselors on our staff, and the complaints from the Student Association were even louder. After observing this for a while, I reconsidered our situation and realized that we had made the problem worse rather than better. I fired all but a few psychologists. I told the Student Association that this was a tough place, like business, and they had better get used to it. That put an end to it."

One challenge about CS&P services is to know how much "capacity" to assign to manage the various CS&P responsibilities of relationships. Whether the "capacity" is small or large, the assigned CS&P people will be 100% busy, much like the counselors at Harvard Business School, since CS&P work will expand to fill the available CS&P capacity.

How much, then, is "just right?"

We've observed how agencies have handled this over the years, and we've developed a pragmatic way of thinking about CS&P headcounts:

CS&P headcounts vary in proportion to SMUs, on the one hand, and to relationship complexity, on the other hand.

Thus, CS&P headcounts vary in proportion to creative headcounts, with the proportion varying up or down depending on relationship complexity:

TABLE 12-2: CS&P HEADCOUNT PER CREATIVE HEADCOUNT

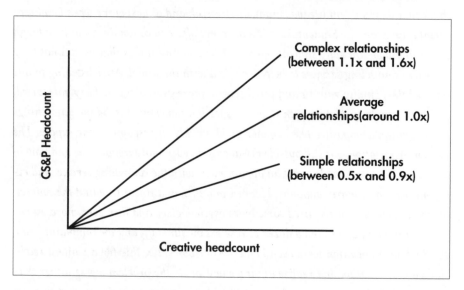

The proportion of CS&P headcounts to creative headcounts can be expressed as a CS&P ratio which varies with relationship complexity. The ratio is the CS&P headcount divided by the creative headcount. If there are, for example, 10 CS&P full-time equivalents and 10 creative full-time equivalents, then the CS&P ratio is one (or 1.0x), and so forth. Simple relationships have a CS&P ratio of between 0.5x and 0.9x; average relationships have a CS&P ratio of about 1.0x, and complex relationships have a CS&P ratio of between 1.1x and 1.6x headcounts per creative. The CS&P ratio has been in decline over the past decade. Just as creative headcounts have declined per SMU under the pressure of declining prices, so has the proportion of CS&P resources relative to creative resources. Typical or average relationships used to have CS&P ratios of 1.5x during the years 1990 to about 2004, but since then, CS&P ratios have declined to 1.0x.

Complexity of a relationship defines the magnitude of the CS&P ratio. Normal responsibilities include carrying out brand strategic work, coordinating the briefing and ad approval processes between a client and the creatives and managing the relationship for budgeting and planning purposes. Highly complex relationships include some or all of the following CS&P tasks that are in addition to normal CS&P responsibilities:

- Integrating the strategic and creative operations of numerous agencies across geographies or media disciplines;

- Managing global operations out of a single agency office, including conducting global brand strategies and all global brand creative work;

- Managing exceptionally high levels of brand strategies and other types of strategic work;

- Managing exceptionally inefficient processes, like inefficient brief approval or ad approval processes;

- Managing exceptionally high rates of rework associated with these processes;

- Managing an exceptionally complicated SOW planning and budgeting or fee-setting process.

It is fair to say that the advertisers are responsible for many of the factors that drive up CS&P ratios, particularly when the high ratios are due to process inefficiencies involving brief approval, ad approval, rework rates and SOW planning or fee-setting. Agencies know this, of course, and try to staff up accordingly rather than work with the client to make relationships more efficient. In the particularly fraught fee-setting environment of today, agencies will happily accept any inefficiencies in a relationship if the inefficiencies justify additional headcount and billable hours.

This is, of course, unfortunate – but labor-based fees encourage rather than discourage relationship inefficiencies, and as long as agencies are paid for these inefficiencies, they are hardly motivated to develop the skills or put in the effort to eliminate them.

CHAPTER 13 – MANAGING SCOPES OF WORK AND PREPARING CLIENT RESOURCE PLANS

"Obviously, some people here do not appreciate the gravity of our situation."

Credit: Frank Modell / The New Yorker / The Cartoon Bank.

If you've read this far, you'll recognize that all the elements are in place for knowing how an ad agency can go about managing its SOWs, client by client, and determining the appropriate resources and fees for its relationships, using the various principles and metrics outlined in this book.

Ideally, of course, this SOW management will be done in sync with engaged clients with whom an agency has previously established *Marketing and Strategic Performance Partnerships* as outlined in Chapter 10. These partnership clients are more likely to pay fairly for agency workloads and resources, believing that agencies are critical partners who contribute in a major way to the achievement of brand growth and profitability. SOW planning and agency resourcing decisions are critical processes in planning for improved performance.

There's a chicken-and-egg problem with clients, though. There are few clients who have these kinds of partnerships with their agencies. Client relationships have been deteriorating for more than a decade, as fees have declined faster than agency workloads, and agencies have been treated more like commodity suppliers of creative execution services than as strategic partners. Clients work with strategic management consultants on issues they deem fundamental and important. Clients have beefed up their own capabilities and lowered their expectations for their agency relationships. Associated with this has been the agency practice of downgrading the cost and seniority of their own resources in response to unfavorable relationship economics. There are many reasons for this, and they have been discussed in previous chapters, but the effect has been a deterioration of relative agency capabilities at a time when their clients face unprecedented difficulties in achieving growth and profitability in the dog-eat-dog competitive world brought about by online commerce.

Agencies have to dig themselves out of the hole they have dug for themselves over the past decade. Their situation is a bit like being on a losing football team, behind in the fourth quarter and needing some last-minute team heroics to come out winning. It's a situation that calls for entirely new strategies: *new ideas and leadership from the top,* bringing fundamental changes in agency management style, operational direction and nitty-gritty attention to detail, uncomfortable as this might be for those more used to the casual, hands-off management culture of ad agencies.

Glorification of past leaders and their management styles is a distraction. Today's conditions require new approaches and an abandonment of the belief that there is any possibility of returning to a time when agencies were exceptionally well-paid for carrying out what was, then, a relatively simple creative business involving TV, print and radio.

Office heads are the essential, key executives for bringing about effective management of scopes of work, whether they be called office president, chief executive, managing director or something else. Traditionally, office heads were once high-status agency executives responsible for new business development, recruiting and client problem-solving in key agency offices (New York, Chicago, London, Paris, Frankfurt, Tokyo, etc.). Office heads needed Mad Man skills to deal with clients during the commission era, but with the evolution of remuneration to fees and the increased importance of global clients in an office's mix of clients, the job has become increasingly managerial and custodial in nature as they struggle to balance fees and resources to achieve holding company margins. The office head is no longer today quite the local god he or she used to be, and with an increasing percentage of global clients, office heads have less control over clients than was the case in the past. Although the office head job is increasingly managerial, *it is not managerial enough.*

The office head can have a greater influence over client operations, influencing client scopes of work and agency resource plans. Office heads have the authority to provide and impose standards on client heads. This is not an authority that has been used to any great extent in the past. In point of fact, office heads have left client heads alone to handle their clients as they best saw fit, rarely looking very closely at what client heads were doing on a day to-day, month-to-month or quarterly basis.

The office head has the singular authority to establish processes and standards for each client head, and it is office head *leadership at the office level* that is required today. Of course, office heads are unlikely to step up to these responsibilities unless they are required to do so by agency chief executives, so it's critical for CEOs to understand the office-level need for increased management, and to direct the agency's office heads to begin the process, as described below.

Office head authority should be used in the following way:

1. **SOW forecasts as a matter of policy.** Office heads must establish a policy that each client head must forecast his/her SOW 'by deliverable' for the office's/agency's fiscal year. If the fiscal year is January through to December, then this must be the period for the client head's SOW forecast, even if his/her client's fiscal year is structured differently – July through June, April through March or on some other basis[24]. Forecasted SOWs represent a stake in the ground: *"this is the work we should do or will be required to do for each client in our coming fiscal year."*

2. **SOWs in a uniform format, permitting calculation of SMUs.** There has to be a uniform template for the SOWs, even if individual clients of the agency specify *their own* unique format for *their* SOWs. Uniformity within the agency is an absolute requirement. At Farmer & Company, we provide our clients with the Farmer SOW Template, which outlines the projects by media type, by media detail, by origination/adaptation and by creative complexity (low, average, high). Additionally, the template specifies if an individual project is creative only, production only or full-up. What's important is that the relevant detail be provided to permit SMUs to be calculated across clients for comparative purposes.

3. **SOWs diagnosed for their "state of health."** The forecasts of SOWs in a uniform format with SMU values permit "state of health" diagnoses to be performed. What is the price for the work in each of the SOWs (fee per SMU)? What are the creative productivities, as measured in SMUs per creative per year?

4. **SOW changes tracked throughout the year.** It's one thing to get a SOW forecast at the beginning of the fiscal year and to use it for diagnostic purposes. It's another thing to see what actually happens. Office heads need to specify that SOWs will be tracked during the year and that changes will be monitored. Our clients use ScopeTrack™, our cloud-based SOW tracking program. ScopeTrack™ incorporates SMU metrics, so it is particularly useful for tracking client-by-client workloads and

workload metrics. ScopeTrack™ users, who are typically in the client service or project management functions, log in weekly and keep track of deliverable changes – added projects, dropped projects, changed projects (changes in dates or complexity); additional rounds of rework, and the like. The reasons for the SOW changes can be entered in a free-form remarks section. When reworks are logged, the reasons for the rework and the client executive responsible for generating the rework can be noted. Not surprisingly, an 80-20 rule seems to apply about rework: 80% of the rework is created by 20% of the clients, and within these clients, 80% of the client rework is created by 20% of certain client marketing executives. It's helpful to have a record of the rework, the reasons for the rework and a list of the client executives who generate the rework. On those occasions where the rework is due to agency work being off-brief, this should be noted, as well, in the interest of accuracy and objectivity. Not all rework is generated by picky client executives or hierarchical approval processes.

5. **Client (and client head) performance reviewed at regular intervals.** Office heads need to demonstrate their commitment to SOW management practices by sitting down with client heads, one by one each quarter (or so), and reviewing their client operations. The following kinds of questions ought to be raised during the reviews:

- What work are we doing for your client? How does our work address the client's brand performance problems? *If not, what can we do about it?*

- Is the client's fee budget and our SOW large enough to deal with its brand performance problems? Do we have enough share of the overall fee budget so that we are the agency that is making a difference in client performance? *If not, what can we do about it?*

- How are we being remunerated by this client? Is workload being considered in the fee calculation? *If not, what can we do about it?*

- How much work is in the SOW – in projects and SMUs? What is the fee per SMU? SMUs per creative? What is our CS&P ratio? *If these metrics are not acceptable (insufficient fee per SMU or stretched resources), what can we do about it?* Clients whose metrics are not acceptable are classified as "misaligned" clients: the fees, resources and workloads are misaligned with one another. There is too much work, too little fee, and too few resources for the work. Misaligned clients are a big problem – recall the Daedalus NY Office from Chapter 8, which had a majority of clients in the "misaligned" category. Misaligned clients need to have corrective action plans developed and implemented by their respective client heads.

- What improvements are you [the client head] prepared to commit to for the rest of this fiscal year? [These commitments need to be negotiated with the office head, ensuring that they are ambitious and realizable].

- What are your three key long-term priorities for the management of this client? Where does the alignment of fees, resources and workloads fit into your priorities?

Any client head who sits through a review of this nature will have little doubt about the importance that the office head puts on effective client and SOW management. Improvements in the performance of clients within the office's portfolio of clients will be expected. Client heads will inevitably feel that they need to be more on top of their client situations, being more pro-active with fees and SOW issues. In other words, they will inevitably feel *accountable* for their client and its relationship with the agency, and under management pressure to do something about existing problems.

Client reviews – or performance reviews, as they ought to be known – are a standard feature of corporate life. *Management*, it is said, is getting subordinates to do what they would otherwise not do on their own. As J Sterling Livingston pointed out in *Pygmalion in Management*, his landmark *Harvard Business Review* article of 1969 (reprinted in 2003), *"If managers' expectations are high, productivity is likely to be*

excellent. If their expectations are low, productivity is likely to be poor. It is as though there were a law that caused subordinates' performance to rise or fall to meet managers' expectations." (Livingston, 2003). The challenge, then, is to get office heads to show their expectations to client heads through the review process. The example set by office heads will raise the performance bar for client heads.

Unfortunately, the culture of the advertising agency has ratified, over many decades, a policy of benign neglect regarding client operational matters. Agency wealth, particularly during The Golden Age, was based not on how well or how closely an individual client was managed but rather on how long a client remained a client of the agency. Commission-based remuneration assured the generation of profits. Increases in agency wealth were generated through new business wins. Understandably, it was the responsibility of client heads to retain their clients, principally by offering great creativity and unrivaled and endless service, and it was the responsibility of office heads to develop new clients. If each party did what was expected, then agencies grew and flourished. This was "ant-colony" management, in the memorable words of Kevin Roberts. Each ant knew what it needed to do – and did it.

Alas, that is not the case today, and the responsibilities of office heads and of client heads have changed. It is not a natural progression for either group of executives to be effective under both the old rules and the new.

6. **Action plans designed and agreed to deal with misaligned clients.**
    Client reviews must lead to action plans – that's the purpose of the exercise, especially for misaligned clients whose poor economics are stressing the agency organization and compromising its ability to do first-class work. If misalignment is due to poor fees relative to workload, then efforts must be undertaken to increase the fees or reduce the workload, using the documentation of workload and SMU metrics to facilitate the discussion.

173

Agencies negotiate with clients all the time over fee levels, seeking re-muneration for out-of-scope work, overtime for rework and annual fee increases for growing SOWs, but their usual justification is the excessive time sheet hours that they incur. Time sheet hours are easily attacked by clients, who argue that excessive hours are merely a symptom of agency inefficiency.

7. **Progress in achieving action plans – reviewed on a regular basis.** Client heads need to organize initiatives and discussions with their clients to promote the achievement of their action plans, and office heads need to inspect the results from time to time. This can take place within the context of regularly-scheduled review meetings or on a more ad hoc basis. What's important is that office heads must be seen as following up with client head commitments, and learning more about the client head's capa-bilities and about the sources of resistance at the client if the client head constantly turns up empty-handed. Out of this process, office heads will certainly learn more about "who can deliver" improvements from their clients. The learnings can be exploited for the benefit of all if aired at routine office board meetings, where the client heads assemble with other senior office executives to discuss office operations.

8. **Best practices discussed and disseminated for training and leader-ship purposes.** Successful client heads should be given airtime and brag-ging rights at office board meetings, revealing what they went through to transform a misaligned client into an aligned client through inter-actions with procurement and marketing. Giving successful executives time and visibility is a way of celebrating success and reinforcing Pygma-lion-in-management practices that encourage all client heads to strive for success with their clients. Collective experience is a powerful force, but it needs to be mobilized. Best practices are routinely shared inside con-sulting firms and at corporations, but they are woefully absent within the advertising agency network.

Best practices could focus on "how I used workload data and other met-rics to bring about a change with my client." Everyone can benefit from hearing successful war-stories, whether the forum is within one office or across agency offices. Best practices help to create winning cultures by exploiting and celebrating success. By contrast, organizations that fail to recognize and mobilize best practice success stories cut themselves off from a valuable asset. A worldwide ad agency, with 10-20 clients per office and 100 offices around the world has 1,000-2,000 local client heads and the wealth of experience that they represent. What would it take to mobilize and disseminate the best practices of this group of individuals and exploit them for the benefit of the agency?

9. **Rewriting advertiser-agency contracts.** Office (and global) contracts need to be upgraded on many fronts. First, contracts should be explicit about the agency role in the relationship. We believe that agencies should be acknowledged as strategic performance partners, as outlined in Chapter 10, and held to the higher standard that this implies – responsible for the joint planning of SOWs that have the highest probability of achieving improved brand results, and managing or coordinating the network of agencies that has been mobilized to provide expertise across all media types. Second, contracts need to be explicit and complete in all areas relating to SOW issues – planning, measuring, tracking, resourcing, remunerating, dealing with out-of-scope and rework issues and the like. It is not enough to declare that an agency is the advertiser's agency of record (AOR) and will carry out strategic, creative and production work in accordance with a SOW. The devil is in the detail. How is the workload of the SOW measured? By what agreed standards is the SOW resourced by the agency for relationship coordination, strategic work, creative work and production? How is the cost or the billing rates of the resources determined? What rewards exist if the agency delivers or over-delivers the expected results from the SOW program? Ad agencies need to have "model" contracts in mind as they manage their relationships towards new contracts and new ways of working with their clients. The effort is long-overdue.

FEES, RESOURCES AND WORKLOADS

The office head sets the tone through personal leadership in the office, and his/her efforts should lead to increased client head accountability for client management practices. From a practical standpoint, though, how should client heads proceed with their clients in negotiating fees and resources from the forecasted SOWs?

Agencies need a uniform way of thinking about these issues. Negotiations with clients are not individual crap shoots by client heads. There's more to success than being charismatic and lucky. The agency needs to make the client head negotiation job easier by adopting certain concepts and approaches that each client head can fall back on, relying on an agency's values, accumulated wisdom and experience to bolster his/her negotiating skills.

Agencies should create an "agency way" as a framework. At Ogilvy & Mather, it would be called "The Ogilvy Way." At Saatchi & Saatchi, it would be called "The Saatchi Way." At TBWA, it would be called "The TBWA Way," and so on.

What are the key principles of an "agency way?" I think that they can be articulated as follows:

- *We believe that our mission is to create sustainable growth and profitability for our clients through our joint marketing efforts.*

- *We believe in the primacy of the SOW. Forecasted and negotiated SOWs are the foundations of our relationship in any given year. They represent our best thinking about what will be required to improve brand performance, and they provide the basis for the allocation of our expert resources that are required to do the job.*

  - *Our SOWs consist of a number of strategic and creative projects whose workload values can be measured in SMUs. Appropriate classification of individual projects is required to generate accurate SMU values. We and our clients will engage in serious and thorough discussions to assure that we jointly agree on the classification of each of the individual projects in our SOWs. The SMU values of our SOWs are the starting points for the determinations of our resources and fees.*

  - *First, our creative resources. Creative headcounts will be determined on an "SMUs per creative" basis, using 4.1 to 5.0 SMUs per creative per year as the* benchmark metric to determine creative headcounts. If a forecast SOW has (say) 50 SMUs of work, then we will negotiate for a minimum of 10-12 creative FTEs, with seniority and skills mix that match the needs of the SOW.

- **Next, our production resources.** Production resources are directly correlated with the size and media mix of the SOW and will be calculated and negotiated accordingly, using our resource calculating model to determine production headcounts.

- **Finally, our CS&P resources.** Our CS&P resources are scaled to the SOW and the nature of our relationships through an appropriate CS&P ratio, which is used to determine the number, seniority and skills of our CS&P resources. We will generally determine our CS&P resources with a CS&P ratio of 1.0x or, where relationship requirements are more complicated, with higher ratios, which will be thoroughly discussed and agreed with our clients.

- Our fees will be determined on the basis of the actual cost of our calculated resources, using contractual formulas that have been agreed separately. Our actual costs are our actual costs, and so we will not accept so-called cost benchmarks proposed by benchmarking consultants, presumably derived from other agencies who have other salary or overhead cost structures.

- We believe in constant evaluation and adjustment of SOWs to optimize results, and as part of our relationship we will evaluate the efficacy of our ongoing programs and will recommend changes in SOWs as required. As a consequence, we will rigorously monitor and track our changing workloads throughout the year, and we will adjust our calculated resources and fees transparently on the basis of the changing SOWs.

- We believe that our relationships should become more efficient over time, and on the basis of our experience with our clients, we will seek to improve the SOW management process, including planning, briefing, ad approval and resourcing. Over time, efficiencies will be reflected in improved resource metrics, like higher SMUs per creative per year, lower production FTEs per SMU, and lower CS&P ratios. We will seek to create improved relationship operations that will permit us *to operate with more efficient use of resources relative to SMU workloads.*

- *Efficiencies are more likely to be achieved where we, as a single agency, are the principal agency partner across all marketing disciplines and geographical areas, and we will strive to achieve such primacy in our relationships.*

Does this seem like pie-in-the-sky thinking?

Agencies complain today that they are treated like junior partners in their relationships, forced to accept excessive workloads, inadequate fees and impossible deadlines. They watch as their clients flirt with other agencies and divide relationships among an increasingly large number of agencies across all disciplines. They observe other advertisers in the industry careen from one agency to another, firing their incumbent agencies and bringing on newcomers for a short period of time before beginning the cycle over again. Agencies think "maybe I had better keep my mouth shut and do whatever I am asked" rather than *articulate requirements for a successful relationship.*

Yes, I suspect that what I have outlined above will seem like the amusing but unrealistic fantasies of a management consultant, completely out of touch with the practical realities of today's agencies, or so it would seem.

Well, maybe so, but current agency strategies of "keeping mouths shut and doing whatever asked" are leading to decay, irrelevance and disaster. That's the path. Agency senior executives owe something more to their organizations than leading them down this path – or, if this is the best they can do, then they should take big cuts in pay. Agency executives should not earn seven-figure pay packages for presiding over the progressive and inevitable weakening and decay of their organizations.

CHAPTER 14 – TRANSFORMING THE AGENCY

Credit: Mick Stevens / The New Yorker / The Cartoon Bank.

Strategic transformations are management's answer to a two-part question:

1. What are our most fundamental problems?
2. What do we have to do to solve them?

That may seem commonsense, but in practice, it's not that simple.

It takes discipline to think about and identify the *fundamental* problems among the range of problems with which an organization is grappling. In the agency world, there are many real problems that can be identified – some are fundamental, and others are symptoms of larger problems. Here's a short list of what is heard and written about today. Some of these are excuses designed to explain away poor performance or weaknesses in the marketplace.

1. **We're insufficiently digital.** *We'd like to be more digital, and we know that we need to be more digital, but we have too few digital people and no particular digital reputation. As a result, we have little digital work from clients and insufficient financial resources to invest in digital capabilities.*

2. **We give away our work.** *We pitch for free and give away our best ideas. We have too much unpaid work. We're paid for some of our hours, but not all of our hours, and the rate that we're paid is a commodity rate. We should be paid for the ideas that we create and sell them at a price that reflects the value of what they're worth.*

3. **Our principal problem is procurement.** *We're great partners with marketing, but our clients have been hijacked by procurement. Procurement buys agency services in the same way that they buy paper and pens, at the lowest price possible. We'd be fine if it weren't for procurement.*

4. **There's no pricing discipline in the industry.** *Our fellow agencies undercut one another to get new business. When we pitch, we're unlikely to get a fair price; there's always an agency that will price lower. It's very difficult to win new business at a fair price.*

5. **Our own organization negotiates poor contracts.** *We're stuck with client contracts with low fees negotiated by the holding company or one of our senior executives. We can't make money on many of our contracts.*

6. **Our creativity seems lackluster.** *Something is missing – our creativity is off the mark. We're not winning new business. We're losing long-term clients. We need to shake up our creativity with new leadership and new energy, and we*

need to look at the creative resources we currently have. Maybe they're simply not up to the mark. We need to reinvest to become more creative.

7. **We lack project management skills.** *Our operations are chaotic, and that's costing us money. We need to invest in project management people and systems to get our operations and costs under control.*

8. **We're not as analytical as we need to be.** *The marketplace requires us to build mass brands in a personalized and fragmented world. We have to develop better analytics to put the focus on delivering improved brand results while not squandering brand equity.*

9. **We're not attracting the right talent.** *Companies like Google, Facebook and Twitter attract millennials by offering strong creative cultures, competitive compensation and the opportunity to make a difference. We're less relevant on these dimensions, especially on salary, and we're losing the battle to hire and retain the best talent.*

10. **We're not reinvesting enough in our culture.** *Ideas are the agency's livelihood and lifeblood. They need to inspire. We need to continue to invest in having the best ideas for our clients and brands. We need to be brave enough to challenge the legacy models of how things have been done to ensure we continue to set the standard for creativity. This requires a conscious investment to maintain and strengthen our culture. We need to get back to the basics of Bill Bernbach. David Ogilvy and Leo Burnett.*

I could go on with this list, but you get the idea.

Let's assume that this is a representative list of top-of-mind industry problems. Many of these are simply complaints – grumbles about an industry that is going in the wrong direction – rather than starting points for corrective action. The complaints can be summarized like this: "*We know what our problems are, but solving them either requires more money, which we do not have, or a change in attitude by procurement or our fellow agencies, which is not likely to happen. Consequently, although we're smart enough to know how we would like things to be, or how they need to be, we have no practical way to get there. We'll just have to soldier on with things the way they are, do the best we can under the circumstances and hope for the best. We'll focus on improving our creativity and winning new business."*

The complaints reflect the industry's two most fundamental problems: inadequate pricing and a lack of management confidence about solutions. Poor pricing prevents agencies from investing in digital and analytical capabilities, and from being able to hire the kind of talent that solves client brand problems in a complicated media world. No amount of investment in project management disciplines will solve these problems. Lack of management confidence condemns agencies to insufficient action and a bleak future. The best agency people will walk away, voting with their feet, making the problems even worse.

Poor pricing is the outcome of past agency decisions on a number of fronts. The agency focus on "creativity" at a time when clients began to obsess about "shareholder value" was one key factor. So was the failure to measure workloads and to accept, instead, hourly-based remuneration as the basis for fixed fees. So was the continued provision of unlimited client service, just like in the good old days, even though it was not affordable. Passivity in the face of the salary-and-overhead benchmarking consultants was an additional factor that corrupted the basis of fee calculations. The absurd notion that there are industry "benchmarked" salaries, overhead rates and profit margins should never have been accepted as a basis for serious discussion between ad agencies and their clients. Many agencies may have lower salaries, overheads and profit margins than Agency A, but this does not mean that Agency A should be compelled to use these metrics as a basis for fee negotiations with their clients. There may be market prices for diamonds, silver and gold, but Tiffany and Kay Jewelers do not charge the same prices. If you want Kay Jewelers' prices, don't go to Tiffany!

Poor pricing is the mathematical outcome of growing workloads and fixed or declining fees, and poor pricing has locked in agency weaknesses. In the 22 years that Farmer & Company has been measuring prices for agency work (in SMUs), we've observed that the price has declined by more than 60% from $400,000 per SMU to $150,000 in fixed 2014 dollars. Understandably, this has affected and weakened agency operations in a significant way.

Poor pricing has eroded agency salaries. At the time of writing, using available salary data from industry sources (see, for example, www.glassdoor.com) we observe that agencies pay new university graduates less than half the going rate paid by Google, Facebook, Twitter or any of the consulting firms – approximately $35,000 for agency starting salaries with no bonuses versus $65,000 (or more) starting salaries with signing bonuses and guaranteed end-of-year bonuses for Google, Facebook, Twitter and the management consulting firms. The higher salaries of this latter group reflect the intense competition among these firms for top-tier graduates, and they reflect, as well, the superior pricing these firms derive from their commercial operations. Taking the consulting firms as the most comparable example, the strategic consulting firms are paid a five times to six times multiple on the costs of their higher-paid people compared to the typical agency multiple of 2.2 times to 2.4 times on lower-paid people. A consulting firm may receive at least $450-$500 per hour for a typical mix of its consultants on an engagement, while a comparable agency will receive $200 per hour or less. Both types of companies, it should be noted, have to deal with procurement for the approval of their contracts and remuneration rates, so procurement cannot be fingered exclusively as the "bad guy."

The pricing problem is the root cause of the very real salary and talent problems, and unless there is a genuine commitment by senior agency executives to improve pricing, one vigorous step at a time, then there is little hope that agencies will acquire the talent to become more relevant for their clients. This is because the pricing problem leads agencies to downsize and juniorize – forms of disinvestment masked by the delivery of profit margins. Because the generation of profits is seen as a good thing – the real objective of agency operations, at least in the eyes of holding company owners – it is hard to recognize the deteriorating situation for what it is. Understandably, agencies have lost a lot of problem-solving credibility with their clients, and this puts even more pressure on pricing.

Poor pricing leads to disinvestment, and disinvestment leads to reduced problem-solving, and reduced problem-solving leads to further poor pricing. This is a classic self-reinforcing feedback loop – a doom loop for agencies – and the industry is caught in the midst of it.

Holding companies, for their part, probably understand this problem, but they are understandably reluctant to acknowledge it or to take visible steps to help their agencies fix it. First of all, any recognition or acknowledgment that their ad agencies are generating profits by squeezing resources would be a tacit acknowledgement that holding company earnings are low quality and becoming lower quality over time. This would not be the kind of information that would shore up P/E ratios or share prices. Second, holding companies are not really organized to provide much help in an operational sense. Holding companies are principally organized as financial entities, good at making acquisitions, imposing new financial controls and budgeting systems, and negotiating budget and profit targets with a huge number of independent portfolio companies. They are financially sophisticated and have grown in financial sophistication. WPP, like the other holding companies, was organized to acquire underperforming ad agencies and provide financial disciplines to help them achieve higher levels of profitability. This required better cost disciplines than the agencies had provided for themselves. JWT earned only a 4% profit margin in 1986, during the height of the media commission days, when (by our calculations) clients were paying something like $400,000 to $500,000 per SMU for agency work (in today's dollars). JWT's poor profit performance was surely evidence of poor cost management in 1986. By contrast, clients today pay only $150,000 and $200,000 per SMU, but agencies routinely generate 15% profit margins under the more rigorous cost-management disciplines brought about by holding companies owners.

Say what you will, the holding companies have brought about a remarkable change in the culture of their agencies. The unfortunate part of this is that the achievement of holding company financial targets has become a principal goal of ad agencies – a goal that trumps, on the basis of current evidence, the agencies' own strategic health.

Excess agency costs have long been wrung out. Our consulting work suggests that most agency SOWs were appropriately staffed in 2004, when agencies were being paid appropriately by their clients for the workloads then being commissioned. Resources and workloads were in balance. In previous years, agencies overstaffed their work, much like T&C Agency. The year 2004 was a brief interlude between the overstaffing of prior years and the understaffing of recent years. Holding companies always sought growing profit margins, but the profit quest since 2004 has had dire consequences. Holding company profit requirements have contributed to the agency downsizing problem – and been a factor in agency disinvestment for the past 10 years.

The real agency problem is not from holding company pressures, though, but from their own managerial passivity in letting workloads get out of control without finding a way to measure them, track them, resource for them and negotiate fees based on them.

The real agency problem resides in the C-suite of ad agencies, and it is to the C-suite that we must turn to find leadership for the required changes. This won't happen unless agency CEOs finally admit that poor pricing is the fundamental problem that must be solved. Agency CEOs have the responsibility to solve the price problem. It's time to get started.

How, then, should senior agency executives begin the process?

If you – the reader – are an agency CEO, then the only way this can get started is if you convince yourself and your agency organization that the current path is unacceptable and cannot continue – it's a dead-end. You must screw up the courage to take organizational risks in overturning the laissez-faire agency culture – a task for which you may feel unprepared. You may have little confidence in yourself about directing the transformation, knowing that uncertain risks are sure to be run. But as an historian once wrote, "A ship in harbor is safe, but that is not what ships are built for."[25] A lack of confidence tells you that you are in the right place – it's the destiny of leaders to have doubts during difficult times but to overcome them to do what needs to be done.

Lou Gerstner, who joined IBM in 1993, certainly had doubts about himself and his prospects as he considered the challenges he would face as CEO:

> *"IBM's sales and profits were declining at an alarming rate. More importantly, its cash position was getting scary... mainframe revenue had dropped from $13 billion in 1990 to a projection of less than $7 billion in 1993, and if it did not level off in the next year or so, all would be lost... I was convinced...that the odds were no better than one in five that IBM could be saved, and that I should never take the position... The company was slipping rapidly, and whether that decline could be arrested in time – by anyone – was at issue.*
>
> *Burke [Jim Burke, an IBM Board Member] introduced the most novel recruitment argument I have ever heard: 'You owe it to America to take the job.' He said IBM was such a national treasure that it was my obligation to fix it.*
>
> *I responded that what he said might be true only if I felt confident I could do it. However, I remained convinced the job was not doable – at least not by me"* (Gerstner, 2002, pp. 15-16).

Gerstner did overcome his lack of confidence to join IBM, of course, and the transformation he affected – turning the giant computer company into an integrated consulting service provider – emerged from his efforts to uncover the reasons for IBM's sales and profit problems. He had no blueprint at the beginning. *"I simply had no idea what I would find when I actually arrived at IBM* (Gerstner, 2002, p. 21). He took the job because he relished the challenge.

To kick off the transformation, let me suggest 10 steps that will start agency CEOs on a positive path. You don't have to believe in all of them at once, but if you start out believing the first one, you're well on your way:

1. **Uncover and accept the fundamental problem**. Do some due diligence, diagnosing SOW workloads, fees and resources by client. You will find that your most fundamental problems stem from declining prices (fees divided by workload), and that past management responses to this decline – cost reductions – have caused a serious deterioration in agency

capabilities. Take this one office at a time. You're likely to find that each of your offices looks something like the New York office of The Daedalus Agency (Chapter 8). In finding and admitting the price problem, you take the first critical step towards identifying appropriate solutions.

2. **Renounce downsizing and disinvestment as responses for your price problems.** Acknowledge that the downsizing and disinvesting approach is inappropriate for the future and must be abandoned. Obtain the support of your parent holding company for this. Cut yourself a deal for a year or two while you work on a transformation. Then, take a deep breath – you've abandoned the past, and it's all new territory for you and your organization from this point onwards.

3. **Commit to a program that will realize improved pricing.** You must commit to putting a floor under agency prices and then taking the necessary steps to increase prices by getting workloads under control and paid for, and then (subsequently) enhancing the value of agency services for your clients to realize better prices for your services.

4. **Measure and track agency workloads.** You must establish a policy that *every client served by the agency will have a documented SOW in a uniform format*, permitting the measurement of workloads on a comparable basis across brands, clients, offices and regions. Your office heads must implement this on your behalf – or else. As a result of the policy, you must invest in SOW management and measurement tools, and require 100% compliance in the use of the tools by agency client heads across the agency network. This will not be an easy matter. Agency personnel are used to ignoring the center – they've rarely been held accountable for compliance, and no one thinks they'll get fired for ignoring senior executive policies.[26] Expect this to be difficult, follow through by introducing sanctions for non-compliance, should all else fail.

5. **Establish clear accountabilities for workload management and metrics among the agency's client heads.** You must reverse decades of loose or absent accountability practices and establish, in a way that is un-

derstandable for all concerned, that client heads will be held accountable for workload management practices, fees and resources.

6. **Establish clear review processes to be conducted by office heads.** Client heads need to be accountable to office heads. Establish a policy that office heads will review client heads on a regular basis, at least quarterly, to examine the alignment of workloads, fees and resources and the progress being achieved at eliminating misalignments among these factors. This will give office heads a new set of responsibilities, and it will significantly increase your "reach" into the organization. Office heads are your key lieutenants, and you need to have them on board for the transformation process. If certain office heads do not want to cooperate in this venture, then sack them. That will help to make it clear that you are serious about your program.

7. **Establish, as a matter of policy, that the agency be paid for all the work it carries out for its clients.** Client heads who are managing misaligned clients will be expected to develop corrective action plans to improve fees. Renegotiations with clients will be undertaken on a serious basis. Senior agency executives will be required to provide support for fee renegotiations. It is a fundamental economic fact that there is more to be gained by being paid for all the work that is done than by attempting, against all odds, to negotiate better salary or overhead terms. Be prepared to drop clients whose fees are entirely inadequate for the work they require. Make it clear that this is the reason the client is being dropped.

8. **Acknowledge and accept that clients are governed by shareholder value concerns, and that the mission of the agency needs to be refocused on helping clients improve brand growth and profitability.** Agency creativity is a factor that contributes to delivering results, but creativity is a factor, not an end in itself. Agency creativity no longer delivers results automatically, as it did during much of the Creative Revolution. It's time to abandon the tired *"we're creative"* marketing positioning associated with the creative paradigm, and to step up to the challenge of saying *"we're committed to delivering results."*

9. **Generate and publish thought leadership about how marketing and advertising delivers results in today's multi-disciplinary world.** Agency websites are devoid of ideas. Where are the White Papers and thought pieces that give current and potential clients food for thought? Which agencies can demonstrate that they think longer and harder about the challenge of brand growth and profitability than their competitors? Which client heads and strategic planners are clear thought leaders within an agency network, as demonstrated by their authorship of insightful papers, perspectives and presentations on issues of current concern to advertisers? By what process does an agency tap into and document its own intellectual insights about marketing and advertising effectiveness for clients – and provide meaningful content for current and potential clients? You need to elevate and expose the fragmented knowledge within your network by making it visible and essential. Knowledge must replace creative awards as the focus of an agency's culture. The potential knowledge-creators, like CS&P executives, must increase their professional ambitions and become trained for the more taxing challenge of identifying client performance challenges and putting together marketing strategies and SOWs that contribute to client growth and profitability.

10. **Upgrade CS&P talent.** Recent efforts to "upgrade" CS&P by replacing a percentage of the people with project managers took agencies in the wrong direction. The upgrading process ought to be designed, instead, to convert CS&P people into business-sophisticated and results-obsessed executives who provide consultative services to clients, solving brand growth and profitability problems. Advertiser strategic needs have been growing in complexity, and the pressures of globalization, the proliferation of brands / line extensions, the growing power of the trade, increased competition, increased consumer price-sensitivity and the growth of internet commerce have made brand growth and profitability more and more difficult to achieve. Agencies, during the past two decades of fee declines and growing workloads, have downgraded the seniority and capabilities of CS&P people because of cost pressures that affected recruiting, entry-level salaries and training. Predictably, a void in brand thought-leadership has been created in the marketplace – and

filled by new competitors: MBA-trained strategy and brand consultants working in blue-chip consulting firms. Inevitably, if this direction is not reversed, then advertisers are likely to opt out of the need to pay for agency CS&P resources (other than for a minimal amount of account coordination and communication) and limit agency services to the provision of creative resources only. Agencies must re-establish themselves on the strategic playing field, and add an upgraded "strategic brand and performance consulting" capability to the front end of their resource offerings. Advertisers will always seek and find solutions for their problems. Agencies will be part of the solution only if they offer capabilities that are valued and competitive when compared to the alternatives that their clients may consider.

The effort will require intensive analysis, exceptional communications, changes in key executives and unwanted commentary from the outside world. Going through a transformation is like weathering a storm at sea – the sooner it is over, the better. Here's Gerstner again: *"I've had a lot of experience turning around troubled companies, and one of the first things I learned was that whatever hard or painful things you have to do, do them quickly and make sure everyone knows what you are doing and why. Dithering and delay almost always compound a negative solution. I believe in getting the problem behind me quickly and moving on"* (Gerstner, 2002, p. 68).

THE REAL NEED IS FOR FOCUSED CEO LEADERSHIP

The recurring theme of this book is that agencies are plagued with growing workloads and declining fees. The workloads are not measured, so the knowledge of this problem is not widespread. It is certainly not among the top 10 problems that agency CEOs would describe today.

This lack of knowledge makes it easier for CEOs to respond to agency profit problems by downsizing. If workload sizes and growth rates were known, CEOs would certainly pause before downsizing.

Agencies need strong CEO leaders who are prepared to grapple with three clear challenges:

1. **The workload challenge**. Agencies must begin to document, track and measure their workloads. This will permit their organizations to do a much more effective job negotiating fees and putting a brake on declining fees.

2. **The mission challenge**. The mission challenge involves rethinking and then repositioning the raison d'être of the agency from "creativity" and "big ideas" to "results for clients." Only through such a repositioning can agencies begin to set a course for higher fees (as measured by billing multiples) and begin to close the "value-added gap" between themselves and the management consulting firms. This cannot be done without a wholesale upgrading of skills, particularly in client service, so training is part of the required mix.

3. **The accountability challenge**. The third challenge involves running the agency like a business and creating a strong sense of accountability throughout the organization, office by office and client by client. The current loose structure, justified somewhat romantically on the basis that "this is what is required to run a creative organization," ignores the fact that creativity is being killed on a daily basis by the very lack of accountability.

These three challenges – workload, mission and accountability are CEO challenges. No other executive in the management structure has the stature and authority to bring about these transformations in these three critical areas.

These are "insider challenges." I rather doubt that an outsider would have the credibility to overturn the agency culture, which is what is called for here. It's an insider's challenge, and if there is a CEO or CEO candidate who can intellectually separate himself or herself from the culture that nourished his/her career, there's a big challenge ahead. Take it on! Disrupt the agency! Don't expect to be applauded! It may not be a lot of fun, but it is what is needed.

In order to arrive there
To arrive where you are, to get from where you are not,
You must go by a way wherein there is no ecstasy

T.S. ELIOT

Take comfort in the fact that if you embark on this journey, with seriousness and commitment, you will most certainly succeed, while others – more cautious, more conservative, more wedded to the past – will surely fall by the wayside.

REFERENCES

Adage Data Center. (2013, June 13). World's 50 Largest Agency Companies.

Barton, R. (1955). *Advertising Agency Operations and Management.* New York: McGraw-Hill Book Company Inc.

Burton, J. (2009). *A Marketer's Guide to Understanding the Economics of Digital Compared to Traditional Advertising and Media Services.* New York: American Association of Advertising Agencies.

Christensen, C. M. (1997). *The Innovator's Dilemma.* Boston: Harvard Business School Press.

Colvin, G. (2001, June 25). The Great CEO Pay Heist. *Fortune Magazine.*

Crystal, G. S. (1991). *In Search of Excess: The Overcompensation of American Executives.* New York: WW Norton & Company.

Dan, A. (June 21, 2012). Advertising Shoots Itself In The Foot. Again. *Forbes.com.*

Denning, S. (2013, June 26). *The Origin of the World's Dumbest Idea.* Retrieved from www. forbes.com: http://www.forbes.com/sites/stevedenning/2013/06/26/the-origin-of-the-worlds-dumbest-idea-milton-friedman/

Dentsu Taps Aegis Executive. (2013, June 28). *Advertising Age.*

Dougherty, P. H. (1986, April 28). *www.nytimes.com/1986/04/28/business/3-way-merger-to-create-largest-ad-agency.html.* Retrieved June 11, 2013, from New York Times: www.nytimes.com

Femina, J. D. (1970). *From Those Wonderful Folks Who Gave You Pearl Harbor.* New York: Simon and Schuster.

Fox, S. (1984). *The Mirror Makers.* New York: Morrow.

Friedman, M. (1970, September 13). The Social Responsibility of Business is to Increase its Profits. *New York Times Magazine.*

Gerstner, L. V. (2002). *Who Says Elephants Can't Dance?* New York: HarperCollins Publishers Inc.

Goldman, K. (1997). *Conflicting Accounts – The Creation & Crash of the Saatchi & Saatchi Empire.* New York: Simon & Schuster.

Haase, A. E. (1934). *Advertising Agency Compensation: Theory, Law , Practice.* New York: ANA.

Hammer M. & Champy, J. (1993). *Reengineering the Corporation: A Manifesto for Business Revolution.* New York: Harper Business Books.

Hegarty, J. (2011). *Hegarty On Advertising: Turning Intelligence into Magic.* New York: Thames & Hudson.

Kiechel, W. (2010). *The Lords of Strategy.* Boston: Harvard Business Press.

Kleiner, A. (1987, November 8). Bare Knuckles on Madison Avenue.
   The New York Times Magazine.

Kleppner, O. (1979). *Advertising Procedure.* New York: Prentice-Hall.

Kuhn, T. S. (2012). *The Structure of Scientific Revolutions.* Chicago: The University
   of Chicago Press.

Levitt, T. (1983). The Globalization of Markets. *Harvard Business Review.*

Livingston, J. S. (2003, January). Pylmalion in Management. *Harvard Business Review.*

Marketers, Agencies, Google Spar Over Brands' Precious Data. (2014, March 18).
   Advertising Age.

Mayer, M. (1959). *Madison Avenue, U.S.A.* New York: Pocket Books, Inc.

McNamara, J. (1990). *Advertising Agency Management.* Homewood: Dow Jones-Irwin.

Mierau, C. (2000). *Accept No Substitutes! The History of American Advertising.* Minneapolis:
   Lerner Publications Company.

N.W.Ayer & Son. (1909). *Forty Years of Advertising.* Philadelphia.

Ogilvy, D. (1983). *Ogilvy on Advertising.* London: Prion.

Parkinson, C.N. (1958). *Parkinson's Law.* London: John Murray.

Popper, N. (2012, June 16). C.E.O. Pay is Rising Despite the Din. *New York Times.*

Porter, M. E. (1980). *Competitive Strategy.* New York: The Free Press.

Porter, M. E. (1985). *Competitive Advantage.* New York: The Free Press.

Porter, M. E. (1990). *The Competitive Advantage of Nations.* New York: The Free Press.

Reichheld, F. F. (1996). *The Loyalty Effect: The Hidden Force Behind Growth, Profits, and Lasting
   Value.* Boston: Harvard Business School Press.

Rubel, I. (1948). *Financial Management and Accounting.* New York: Funk & Wagnalls Company
   with Printers' Ink Publishing.

Singer, N. (2012, April 12). In Chief Executives' Pay, A Rich Game of Thrones.
   New York Times.

Stern, C. W. & Deimler, M. S. (2006). *The Boston Consulting Group On Strategy.* Hoboken: John
   Wiley & Sons, Inc.

Stewart III, G. B. (1991). *The Quest for Value.* New York: Harpercollins.

Sullivan, L. (2012). *Hey Whipple, Squeeze This!* Hoboken, NJ: John Wiley & Sons, Inc.

Sutherland, A. B. (2012, April 27). Nice Work if You Can Get It. *Daily Mail.*

Tungate, M. (2007). *Ad Land.* London and Philadelphia: Kogan Page.

WPP. (2003). *Annual Report.* London.

ENDNOTES

[1] As used in this book, *workloads* refer to the creative and production deliverables that represent an ad agency's output for its clients. Included in the workload is the associated brand strategic work that provides "positioning" for the actual deliverables. Creative workloads exist across all media, including TV, print, radio, out-of-home, direct, promotion, sponsorship, digital, social, and every other possible medium that can contain marketing content.

[2] I will frequently use the terms "downsize" and "downsizing." By this I mean "*headcount adjustments that do not keep up with changes in workloads*." This includes staffing reductions in the face of flat workloads; zero staffing growth for growing workloads, or modest staffing growth for substantial growth in workloads. "Downsizing," as used here, always leads to increased stretching of agency resources for a given amount of work.

[3] Industry estimates of relationship longevity are at a new low – four years or so, according to The Bedford Group, although *Campaign* magazine (UK) puts the figure at below three years.

[4] Moore's Law, which originated around 1970, states that processor speeds, or overall processing power for computers doubles every two years.

[5] A typical creative team for TV, print and radio ads consisted of one copywriter and one art director who worked closely with one another on all their projects or 'briefs'. Multiple teams could be assigned by the executive creative director to work competitively on a brief to generate more ideas. Each creative team strove to be the one whose ideas were incorporated in the final ad. Obviously, multiple teams were possible only if there was money to support the extra resources.

[6] A "brief" is a creative project assigned to an agency by its client. An agency "is briefed" to carry out strategic and creative work, leading in most cases to the production of an ad. The document used to brief the agency is called "the brief." *Brief* is synonymous with *project*, and both terms are used interchangeably in this book.

[7] USA Today described Della Femina as "the most colorful creative guy in an industry full of colorful creative guys." (May 17, 1994).

[8] Ignition One was allowed to buy itself out of Dentsu in a management buy-out in July 2013.

[9] A "full-service" ad agency offered creative services (development and production of ads)

and media services (media planning and buying). Both of these services were paid for by the traditional 15% media commission. When the media services were spun out, what was left was the agency's creative services (creatives, production, client service and strategic planning). The spin-off required a change in the way agencies were remunerated, both for the separate media operations and the remaining creative
services operations.

10   Salary "benchmarks" were provided by specialized benchmarking consulting firms who worked on behalf of advertisers. The benchmarker's business was to examine the salary and overhead costs of advertising agencies and find ways to justify cutting their fees. They did this by comparing the costs of the agencies they were investigating to their own "benchmarked cost data." As a matter of practice, the benchmarking firms retained the agency data they gathered during their inquiries and repackaged the data selectively into their benchmark database to be used with subsequent clients. Benchmarking was a highly successful but ethically questionable business, all the more so because the benchmarkers never revealed the source or accuracy of their benchmarking databases. Procurement departments sought out and supported benchmarking firms. Agencies, for their part, tended to believe that many of the salary and overhead benchmarks were pure inventions designed to justify fee reductions.

11   See, for example, www.bain.com; www.bcg.com; and www.mckinsey.com for examples, looking under industry expertise for consumer marketing, media & entertainment, retail or the equivalent.

12   Bruce Henderson published BCG's *Perspective* on The Experience Curve in 1973 and on The Product Portfolio in 1970.

13   Bill Bain's principles, designed to create successful long-term relationships: *1) We must have a three- to- five hour private meeting with the CEO, during which time we will explain our strategic concepts and why they are successful, and he will share with us his aspirations, concerns and fears about his corporate performance. 2) The CEO must be open to the concept that our mission must be to help him improve results through a top-down CEO/Bain-led program that begins with his most important businesses and continues throughout his portfolio. 3) He must be open to the idea that the relationship will last as long as Bain & Company continues to generate positive results that are a substantial multiple of its fees – it is not a short-term budget-limited project-based relationship like those that exist between most consulting firms and their clients. 4) The CEO must agree not to work with Bain's competitors, and Bain will agree not to work with the client's competitors.*

Source: the author's memory – the principles were not written down.

It should be pointed out that these principles were in effect from 1973 for about 20 years, but they were abandoned after Bill Bain left Bain & Company in the early 1990s, since it was believed that they were no longer needed to sell new business or retain clients for long-term relationships.

[14] Direct mailing lists have been around a very long time. The analysis and selection of targeted mailing lists from broader databases was an early form of big data – useful for soliciting magazine subscriptions, credit cards, donors for fundraising, etc. These were closely followed by customer relationship management (CRM) databases and the ubiquitous loyalty programs that subsequently developed. Technology and customer databases have continued to evolve since then, and although big data, as it exists today, dwarfs these early incarnations of customer data analysis, we shouldn't forget about the family resemblance. Big data is a product of evolution, not of recent divine creation.

[15] If you divide client service and planning FTEs by creative FTEs you get what I call the client service and planning ratio – a measure of client service and planning *intensity* relative to client workload (with the creative headcount as a surrogate for the client workload).

[16] Note that in 2005, there were 1.4 briefs in each SMU (479 divided by 340), whereas in 2013, there were 3.2 briefs per SMU (1,506 divided by 465). The 2013 mix of briefs was less "complex," with a higher percentage of lower-workload adaptations and originations of low creative complexity. Despite this simplification of the briefs, the total volume of work in SMUs grew by more than one-third over the eight-year period.

[17] Procurement ignores the fact that holding companies are diversified portfolios, with a heavy weight of media companies in the mix. Strong media profitability, particularly from programmatic buying, are hiding the less stellar profit performance of traditional advertising agencies. Nevertheless, pointing out the strong profit growth of holding companies is an effective negotiation ploy when agency fees are being discussed.

[18] According to a vote of more than 1,000 DDB employees around the world in 2011, this particular quote (*"Nobody counts the number of ads you run..."*) is Bill Bernbach's " number one quote of the century." http://www.ddb.com/BillBernbachSaid/why_bernbach_matters/deep-influence.

[19] "Ants aren't smart," says Deborah M. Gordon, a biologist at Stanford. "Ant colonies are." One key to an ant colony is that no one's in charge. No generals command ant warriors. No managers boss ant workers. The queen plays no role except to lay eggs. Even with half a million ants, a colony functions just fine with no management at all. It relies instead upon

countless interactions between individual ants, each of which is following simple rules of thumb. Scientists describe such a system as *self-organizing*. http://ngm.nationalgeographic.com/2007/07/swarms/miller-text.

[20] Organizational research shows that collaborative decision-making yields improved results over individual decision-making. See, for example, research from the "survivor training series" offered by Human Synergistics International and other training organizations. http://www.humansynergistics.com/ResourceCenter/ResearchandPublications.

[21] Bruce Henderson, founder of The Boston Consulting Group, was a creative thinker and prolific writer. During the early years of BCG, he penned a number of provocative articles and mailed them to potential clients, calling them "Perspectives" – an early version of what we now identify as a blog. The Perspectives were reprinted in 2006 as *The Boston Consulting Group On Strategy*, edited by Carl W. Stern & Michael S. Deimler (Stern CW & Deimler MS, 2006).

[22] If we had included *all rework* as part of our SMU value, rather than "gold standard" levels of rework, then the amount of work in 1992's SOWs would have been higher, and the calculated creative productivity would have been much closer to three ads per year.

[23] Parkinson's Law: The Pursuit of Progress (London, John Murray, 1958)

[24] I've seen many agency offices where each client head kept some form of rudimentary SOW record on the basis of his/her client's fiscal year, and every client head had a different system, but if you tried to add them up in some way to see the office's workload for *its* fiscal year, you could not do so. Most office heads are unaware of the client-by-client workload and of the workload of the total office. In many ways, SOW documentation is no better today than it was when we first encountered it in 1992. The industry has not shown very much progress on this important dimension.

[25] *Salt from My Attic* (1928), The Mosher Press, Portland, Maine; cited in The Yale Book of Quotations (2006) ed. Fred R. Shapiro, p. 705. There are numerous variants of this expression.

[26] I've observed this many times. In one example, the CEO of the European Region of a global ad agency promulgated a written policy that required all European office heads to document all local client briefs in an agreed SOW template. The German office head called me by phone and asked me to pass on a message to the Regional CEO. "*Tell _____ to go f**k himself*," he said. I reluctantly passed on the message. The office head got away with it – he never filled out the template, and he certainly continued in his job.

22 years

building on our success

- 1993 Madrid
- 2007 Barcelona
- 2008 Mexico DF & Monterrey
- 2010 London
- 2011 New York & Buenos Aires
- 2012 Bogota
- 2014 Shanghai & San Francisco